LOVE, EMPATHY, AND PROJECT MANAGEMENT

ROHIT ROMLEY

Made with ♥ on the Notion Press Platform
www.notionpress.com

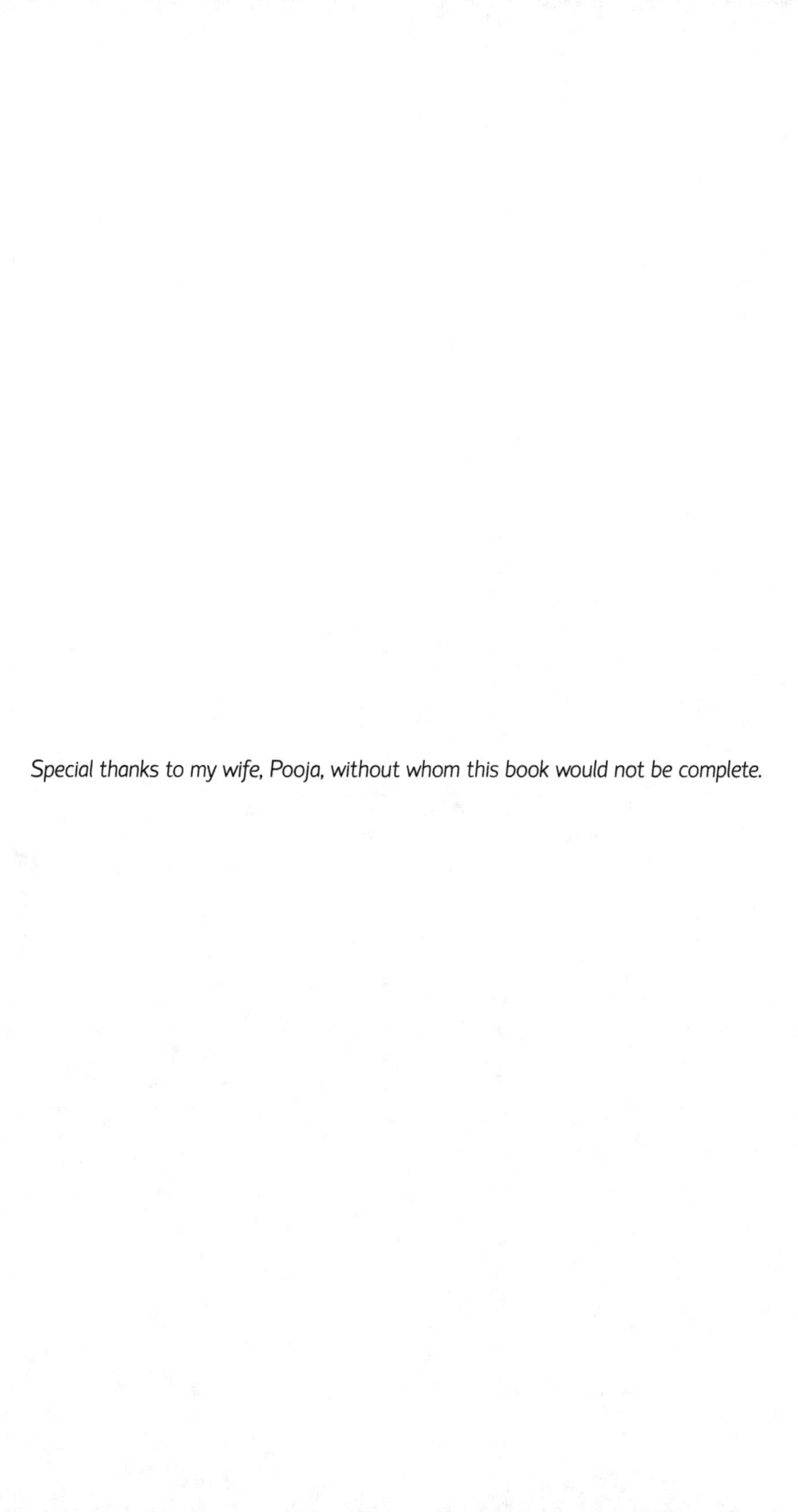

Special thanks to my wife, Pooja, without whom this book would not be complete.

Contents

INTRODUCTION

Enter Caption

If you have picked up this book, it is most likely that either you are a project manager, looking for a pathway to further your career in the field or you are a keen entrant in the market, eager to make an everlasting first impression.

Whatever the reason, congratulations! You have just made the right choice because this book will offer you a comprehensive guide on what project management is all about, and how you can become a successful project manager. This book will also equip you with information about the modern project managing software. This knowledge will prove very critical for you as you set your foot in the competitive and rapidly evolving field of project management.

What is This Book About?

Effective project management is an integral part of a successful project. Project management is a discipline that is both an art and science. Whether you are a project manager, someone starting their new project, or a part of the project team, this book is created to help you understand the practical side of project management and help you effectively work, manage or lead projects successfully.

As a project manager, there is always so much to do. The probability is that you are often overwhelmed by the many responsibilities that fall into your share. You never know where your territory begins and when you are wading into deep murky waters. But as you near the end of the book, you will realize the pillage of your responsibilities does not end till the project is officially closed.

But if you are not careful, you might find yourself going round and round in a loop, doing similar things repeatedly. You find yourself starting things late. You get stuck in loops, unending loops.

Surely, you have started hyperventilating by now thinking of the many challenges you might face during the course of the project but breathe! Once you read through this book, you will realize that a strict adherence to the processes and an innate respect for the people involved in the process will swiftly pave your path to success.

Have you ever wondered how some people are doing the same things, with even lesser resources, and are still timely and effective?

The answer is "Project Management." Project Management is the key to effective performance in this case. If you are a beginner, your first question is what to do.

What is Project Management and Who is a Project Manager?

These questions hold a whole fount of wisdom within themselves. Understanding them helps you lay a solid foundation on your career as a project manager.

How is project management different from management and how is a project manager different from a manager? The entire summary lies in the word "project."

To cut the long story short, here is a simple definition of what project management is:

Project management is the art of leading a team of professionals with different skill sets to the completion of a project, bound by constraints of time, budget and deliverables.

If you have not had your first encounter with project management, you may be perceiving it as an easy challenge, that involves having to abide by time and budget but it is a great test of your managerial skills.

The operations and the objectives of a project vary greatly from the businesses' main operation and thus the challenge lies in using the available resources efficiently and systematically to win against the race of time and constrained budget. The goal of the project is to satisfy the client on their given list of requisites. Often, the client will approach you with an unclear picture of the goal, and overexcited ambitions. Thus, your job begins from first constructing a proper vision for the project and defining in clear terms the deliverables and their smaller components. The deliverables can include the launch of a new product or service, the rebranding of an existing product or the business entirely, or the feasibility of the businesses' expansion and the course to go about it. These are just a few examples of what a project could be, however, the whole list of what your next project could be is endless.

To say every project is unique with its own nature and challenges will not be an exaggeration. Here lies the test of a true project manager. You can never boast that you have got complete command over your niche or that you have gained all the exposure in this domain.

Each project will be a test of your persistence and risk management skills. Not only is each project distinct in its requirements but it is also possible that with each project, you will be expected to work with a different team. If you think you have made exceptional bonding with your current team and understand each other through gestures alone, your companionship may last only as long as the project. Thus, as a project manager you are also expected to be a wonderful mentor and a people's person, to easily gel with all your subsequent project teams. The secret to the project's success lies in a well-managed and a well-integrated team.

So, think of a time when you struggled with the many questions;

What do I do first? Where should I start? Who should I speak to first? Or What should I finish first?

The "What" of what you will do and the "How" of what you will do when you start your very own "first project." You have a lot of questions swimming in your head, making you feel like you are drowning in a sea of confusion. Don't panic. This is normal, especially since you are just getting started.

The reasons for a project's doom can be aplenty but they all point to improper project management. As a project manager, you are the one entirely responsible for your project's success or failure. A good project manager can take an average team to great heights while an unorganized and unaligned PM can bring the whole team down.

Every project with a set vision deserves the best efforts put into it. You will have to engage in your work with the right mindset, skills, and tools required to achieve success in your project!

Thus, it would be best to have project management for yourself, your organization, and your environment.

An average Project manager faces many challenges, especially with that of time, budgets, resources, and workforce. It's not very new to hear a project manager being forced to handle unexpected deadlines, excessive assignments, and the extra burden of team rotations.

According to a study by Harvard Business Review,

> *" One in every six projects costs more than 200 percent of the estimated amount and about 70% of IT projects face project delays".*

And who can forget the large projects of Euro Disney and Boston's "Big Dig" that cost more than double their estimated project cost?

What turns these projects into a "Challenge"?

The answer to this is not that simple. I suggest you read the book and decide.

What to expect when you read this book?

This book will take you **step by step** through the basics of project management. It will answer initial questions about what project management is and guide you through different phases of a successful project. It will introduce you to essential tools of PM like the Gantt chart and modern Project Managing software like Jira. This book provides an interactive insight into the world of PM by offering anecdotes of fictional characters overcoming challenges during the project and handling it. This approach makes for effective learning as you see critical lessons embodied through the stories of fictional project managers. The purpose of using anecdotes is to present complex situations and circumstances through simplified examples, focusing on one aspect alone and letting you absorb the lesson to aid you in your project management journey.

As you reach a more advanced level of understanding, the book will also introduce you to real life examples of projects to reaffirm your understanding of the key concepts.

The book uses an easy-to-understand language to pull you into the world of project management without bombarding you with incomprehensible jargons. As you read further, you will be introduced to key terms of the project management world and then, once you have obtained an understanding of these terms, are the terms used again and again to add them to your vocabulary. Not only will this book introduce you to project management, but it will also make you innately familiar with all its processes so that you can begin your journey in project management without further ado.

The book will also introduce you to different characteristics essential for becoming a good project manager as per the latest market trends. This knowledge often comes with years of experience but in this book, you will find a plethora of information that would allow you to leap through years of experimentation to start your journey smoothly without facing pitfalls. You will have an opportunity to rebuild yourself according to the demands of the present job market, and you will have all the right keywords to add to your resume as you set out to pitch for your first job.

A series of tag questions throughout the book will test your understanding of everything that is being taught so that you can cross check your understanding before moving forward. This book is essentially a teacher. Try to stop and reflect when you are faced with these tags as they will allow you to evaluate understanding. Consider it another safeguard before you set out to learn project management through practice in the field.

You are now all set to begin this interactive read into the world of project management so brace yourself. Here is a brief revision for you about what a project is to propel you towards the next chapter.

A project is simply an undertaking that has a start and the desired end. Unlike plain "management" project management is time and goal bound. It begins with project initiation and ends with the project closure, and consequently the team also comes into being with the project and dissolves with the end of it. Thus, it poses more challenges than normal management and breeds the unique position of a project manager.

A Project Manager is trusted with the responsibility to lead the project team to achieve project goals and to attain client's satisfaction. The next chapters will now take you through the entire project management journey as a process and discipline.

It could be the lack of skills, or lack of clarity of business objectives, poor plans, or simply poor project manager's leadership but it's better you decide when you are done reading it.

A project is simply anything that has a start and a desired end. For instance, building a product, software, or even a workshop is a "Project."

Project Management is the process of leading your teamwork to achieve project goals. So, the primary purpose of this book will be to take you through the entire project management journey as a process and discipline. With visual illustrations, this book gives you a basic understanding of the real purpose it has in practical life.

A project manager understands the needs of the project and then ensures its success. Before you start, you will have to own your goals and be passionate about them. You start with a simple question asking yourself, " Why am I starting this project, and what outcomes am I expecting? The next thing you do is plan the time and cost for your project milestones. The third is you looking after every activity that helps you achieve your objectives. And last is to check the quality of what you produce. By far, this book will define what, who, when, and how you will reach the end of your project.

It will help you and your team take the lead and take control. So, let's get started!

EMPATHY

Enter Caption

Have you ever wondered why we human beings are wired to observe even the tiniest thing that happens around us?

We read into people's thoughts all the time.

You get to your office and notice the happy security guard welcoming you. You glance at the receptionist; her face tells you she is off to a good start today.

The next day, you run late into a meeting, and you notice your client and co-workers waiting for you, not happy with your absence. What allows us to notice these things? The answer is Empathy.

What is Empathy? To put it simply:

"Empathy is the ability to understand people emotionally without judging them, without having any biases."

Imagine if you are running late to work for some reason. When you reach your office, you find unhappy co-workers, making you feel worse about getting late. In such a situation, what would you have wanted? Would you have wanted someone to ask you if everything was alright kindly? Maybe there was a pressing issue at home or on the way that forced you to get late? Maybe you just had a bad night and are feeling mentally drained?

In such a situation, _hearing your co-workers or supervisor say, "I understand you got sick and couldn't complete the work,"_ would make you feel better than, _"I am disappointed that you couldn't complete the work._ and weren't on time today."

Empathy allows you to forge meaningful and deep connections with family, friends, colleagues, and even strangers. Acting in a way that you are empathetic of other people's feelings goes a long way. It enables you to be kinder and greatly improves your interpersonal skills.

A good leader knows to strike a balance between being firm and empathetic with their subordinates. After all, empathy contributes to your emotional intelligence, which is crucial in developing your personal and professional growth.

Empathy also gives you the ability to instantly discern a grin or a smirk on someone's face and understand if anyone around you is struggling in their life. All you have to do is step out of your world and walk into theirs. Try to understand where their feelings stem from. Whether you are a manager or leader or a co-worker, empathy helps you think for others, predict their next move, and learn to make better decisions at every stage of life. It is one of the important skills every leader must possess.

Emotional Intelligence

Emotional Intelligence is one's ability to feel, understand, and apply the knowledge of emotions to connect and influence others.

How do you deal with problems in a company? What do you do when a crisis occurs, and you need to manage it? In all honesty, your behavior and approach say a lot about your EQ. You can start by asking yourself these questions;

- Do you ask questions and try to understand the situation first, or do you feel disappointed in your team?
- Do you look for solutions first, or criticize your team for not doing a better job?
- Do you speak compassionately to your colleagues and respect their contribution to the company despite their failure at executing a task properly?

Your answer to these will demonstrate how emotionally stable you are and how effective you will be with leadership, especially in the capacity of a manager.

At any workplace, you will encounter various situations that are critical and difficult to manage. You might feel pressured by your superiors, and despite having done everything right at your end, things might go wrong because someone else from your team botched up their job. In such circumstances, it is difficult to navigate your role as a project manager or a leader.

What do you do? What should you do? What is the appropriate reaction that is fair and empathetic?

Let's consider this scenario.

Hannah works for a content writing firm as a project manager who leads a five-person team of content writers. She has received a new order from the company's sales team that needs to be urgently delivered because the client has paid a sizable sum.

She lines up two writers from her team, explains the task to them, and gives the editor a heads up about the edits she will have to quickly make to deliver the order on time. Everything is lined up perfectly, and she lets her superiors and sales team know that your team will deliver the task on time.

The next day, she is sipping on her cup of tea as she comes into work, scrolling through new emails when she sees that one of the writers, Sam, has sent her an email. She takes a quick look and realizes that Sam has not started on her part of the task and is asking questions that you had already answered in your meeting yesterday.

Hannah feels a mix of anger and worry that knot together in her chest. She types out a quick email answering Sam's queries once again and urges Sam to meet the upcoming deadline without compromising on the quality of work. Due to Sam's delay, she has a small crisis to handle now. If the task is not completed on time, Hannah will be held answerable for the delay, and it will also reflect badly on her.

She sits down for a moment and thinks through all her options. She gets the editor and another writer on board to help Sam out. Setting a strict deadline for them, she firmly lets them all know that she expects them to do a great job despite the time crunch. This is her attempt to reel in all her resources to deal with the crisis effectively.

The next thing she does is notify the sales team and her boss of an unexpected delay. She requests a small extension and apologizes for the inconvenience. Once she has taken the other stakeholders into the loop, she heads over to her team and supervises the progress closely.

Fortunately, everything goes smoothly after that. The task was delivered a little late, but the sales team communicated with the client about the slight delay, and the client politely accepted the issue. Although Hannah feels relieved, she knows she will have to answer her boss about this delay and be told that it shouldn't happen again.

Knowing all this, she calls in Sam for a small meeting. There are two ways she can approach this situation, but she knows that she has one course of action that will be most appropriate as a good leader. She gestures for Sam to sit down on the seat across her table.

"Hello. I am going to get a cup of tea for myself, do you want me to order something for you as well?"

Sam looks a little hesitant but says, "Just a glass of water will be fine, thank you."

Hannah smiles kindly, getting up to pour Sam a glass of water. She sits down, clasping her hands, and then asks, "So I see there was a bit of a delay on your end for yesterday's task. I remember clarifying all the details to you earlier but there seemed to be a gap in understanding. That's alright though. Is everything alright on your end?"

Sam looks down guiltily and then replies after a small pause.

"Everything is alright on my end. My sister is going through a divorce and I was just mentally occupied with everything so I was unable to concentrate on what you said in the meeting earlier. I am really sorry about it. I will make sure it does not happen again."

Feeling a bit sorry for Sam, knowing that it must have been a difficult time for her, Hannah nods in understanding.

"I understand that. Everyone has difficult situations that come up from time to time. However, I do expect you to let me know when you think it's a bad time for you to work on an important task right now. I will not think any less of you for it. Rather, I will appreciate the heads up. I want to keep my team with me for a long time, and I want you to be comfortable enough to judge your situation and let me know when the pressure might be too much for you to handle. Just a little proactive attitude and honesty will save us all the trouble in the future."

Sam looks up, surprised but grateful at what Hannah has said.

"Yes you are right. Thank you for understanding. I regret the inconvenience the delay must have caused you."

Hannah smiles, "That's alright. We always have lessons to learn. I hope everything gets better for you and your sister. If you need any help, let me know."

Once Sam leaves, Hannah reflects on the situation. Time and time again, it is said that work and personal life need to be strictly separate. Your personal life should not affect your work performance and vice versa. However, this is far from reality. People always have personal struggles that come in their ability to function normally during working and non-working hours.

It is better to create a manager-employee relationship that allows better workflow without compromising workplace satisfaction to sustain a team. Hannah cut Sam some slack but successfully figured out a solution that could prevent a similar issue from occurring in the future.

By making sure you are empathizing with your team and treating them with compassion, you will create an environment that fosters workplace loyalty. Learn to be flexible and find solutions that cater to the needs of your team without compromising on your business objectives. Even in your personal life, a compassionate and empathetic attitude will help you tackle all the challenges that life brings you. Once you learn to understand other people's emotions better, you will build meaningful relationships with people who support you and make you feel valued.

How Managing Empathy and Emotional Intelligence Can Help Conflict Management

Do you watch cricket on television? You must have noticed yourself going ecstatic over the play. Sometimes the player catching the ball makes you feel like you caught the ball yourself. It's pretty natural. Many people experience mirrored emotions, i.e., they reflect the energy they surround themselves with.

Similarly, as a Project Manager, you will find yourself connecting to your team, especially when they are struggling with deadlines, unexpected changes, disgruntled customers, or tough vendors. You will be handling your teams intelligently to get the output that leads you to success.

To become a better Project Manager, you must utilize the essential skill to help you achieve your goals, i.e., "Empathy."

If you never tried it, try now, and you will be surprised to see the results. It will help you to get in tune with your team and your clients too. Remember, if you understand the people you work with, they will trust you, and automatically your communication and work delegation will get smoother.

But how can you manifest this in your attitude while acting as a Project Manager?

Start developing a customer-centric approach

How can you do that?

Understanding your customer's needs is amongst the first and most important rules for any business, and if you don't abide by it, you won't last in the market for a long time. Therefore, a Project manager needs to be aware of the customers' needs and stay informed and connected. More than the brand or product value, customers usually look for someone who can listen to their problems, provide innovative solutions, and support them.

Being a Project Manager, you can manage conflicts proactively by validating your customer's frustrations when they have bad experiences and are dissatisfied due to technical delays in delivery, issues with product or service quality, etc. There can be a time when your customer expects you to stop the project or probably re-align your team and re-engineer the entire process. You will have to sit and sort things out until your customers are on board with your decision.

Similarly, your communication also plays a vital role in keeping your customers happy. Ensure transparency in your operations by checking in with your customers and keeping them updated about what you have to offer. You should always be on top of initiating clear communication by ensuring your client is regularly contacted at their preferred time.

Sometimes clients put forward requests that can be a little too much of an adjustment on a project manager. Again, the trick is not to judge them but give them sufficient time and empathize before you accept or disapprove of any request. Because your client can also be struggling with pressures from their workplace, a little understanding from your side will give them the comfort that they need to build a trusting relationship with you. This type of attitude will go a long way in ensuring that your client will feel comfortable to prefer seeking you out in the future.

Therefore, you will actually be investing in earning their trust and building long-term relationships by showing empathy. So, as an empathetic project manager, you will benefit from building customer trust. Your customers will stay happy, and in return, your company will stand out in their minds, which will give you the much-needed competitive edge in the market.

As a project manager, taking their comprehensive customer feedback, empathizing, and praising your employees will pave your path to success. Don't forget; a happy employee makes happy customers!

Your next focus should be to create a comfortable workplace environment.

According to a report by Gallup, "Employee engagement leads to happier customer relations and in return increases sales by 20%." [1]

Again, the vital thing to do here is to take care of your team and look out for their best interest by staying alert. You should always be an accessible and approachable manager, someone your team wants to discuss their problems with. This way, you will resolve any conflicts, technical issues, and logistical problems. You will also motivate your team and keep their focus on achieving project goals. Eventually, your project will enjoy the success it deserves!

Being empathetic will also help in creating a fair working environment for your team. When you feel for your team, you will assign achievable tasks, and you will constantly be delegating work to people according to their skillset and workload. This will keep your team energetic and will also keep their spirits high.

Thus, your team's weaknesses will be transformed into strengths, which will give a competitive edge to your projects. For instance, there are always people who are introverts and extroverts. As a project manager, you must use everyone's qualities and traits to your benefit but assign them roles they can excel at.

While an emotionally intelligent project manager will be aware of his team's weaknesses and strengths, they will also be good at regulating their own emotions. Consider a company where a new program has been installed. The change will lead to a disruption in the usual flow of information and processes entirely. An emotionally intelligent manager will take along their team and accept the change and learn quickly instead of resisting it. This type of thinking and decision-making will save the organization valuable time and effort.

Emotional Intelligence can help you accept changes and deal with conflict effectively. It also increases your ability to tap into sustained productivity levels. Furthermore, you will strengthen your relationships at work and create a strong bond with your team, customers, and other stakeholders.

Not only does a project manager understand the strengths and weaknesses of their team, but they also know how to strike a balance between team-centered values and achieving business goals. As a project manager, you need to use the strong team management skills learned from polishing your interpersonal, conflict resolution, and rapport-building skills. Once you can connect with your team at a personal level – a level where your team wants to grow with you and for you – you will notice many changes in your team's success. Team loyalty can allow you to raise the efficiency of any project to the best possible level. You must learn how to use people, their skills, and tools – all combined with each other – to give you the desired output that matches your project vision.

Try to provide your team creative freedom and the space to innovate. This will make your team feel a strong sense of responsibility.

By giving people more autonomy, you will notice that they will become more motivated and passionate at work. Imagine a situation where you don't directly acknowledge the importance of a team member to the project they are working on. If you were in a similar position, how would you feel? Won't it be much better if your team lead or supervisor makes you feel important and needed? Of course, it will. A small, worthless acknowledgment in today's times about the fact that your work matters will go a very long way. If you are a project manager who does not reassure his team members about the importance of their roles in the team, what do you think will happen? Will your team lose interest or feel less invested in everything that is happening? The answer is probably. If you don't learn to fix the root of the problem, then the project will meet its failure soon.

Imagine finding yourself in a situation where your Project Manager cries out to their employees, "You people don't seem to do anything right. I will have to revise the team plan or maybe hire someone else to do this job."

It will dampen your spirits and make you feel disposable instead of feeling like a valued member of a team. Knowing this, when the time comes, and you become a leader with your own team, you must remember what you must not do.

Don't be a manager who is temperamental and fitful. Ensure that you are well-respected by your team and not just feared by them.

Take a look at the scenario and decide for yourself. Who do you think is better?

A Project manager cried out to his employees, "You people don't seem to do anything right. I will have to revise the team plan or maybe hire someone else to do this job." In contrast, an emotionally intelligent Project Manager said, "The main problem with your project is that it will foreseeably take longer, which will increase incremental costs. Therefore, I would suggest you revisit the design specifications of the software in a way that it can be achieved in a short time." Thus, this made his team look into its work a little more critically with a solution-oriented approach. It created positive reinforcement and a drive to do better.

Thus the emotionally intelligent project manager acted as a much better leader rather than making his team feel criticized, helpless, and unmotivated.

Similarly, Emotional Intelligence equips the project manager with the skill to manage conflicts better. As you become self-aware, you are open to accepting your emotions, along with others. This allows you to handle disputes and disagreements by finding easy and convenient solutions for everyone. In the end, you will build a supportive team which will affect their morale and the quality of their work. By using effective communication means, you will reduce the hurdles that emerge during a project.

CHAPTER THREE

SUCCESS

Enter Caption

Unlock the real purpose of life

Each one of us has goals we are striving for. Some people want to get rich, and others want to make people happy. Each person has a story to tell.

The question remains, "Is your story interesting enough that people would want to read it?" Is your life interesting enough that people would aspire to have something similar? You should aspire to live a life that inspires others.

You should strive to bring your dreams to reality.

Do you remember the innocent fascination that lit up your eyes as children when you heard stories about all the trials and triumphs of the young Hercules?

You must have read about all the mythological beings and heroes of ancient Greece embarking upon journeys of self-discovery. They would often emerge victorious in their trials – coming out wiser and stronger than before.

In real life, most of us don't get to take a sabbatical from our lives and battle our demons. You don't get a decade-long vacation to figure out who you are or what you want from life. There is no great war to win and no fantastic realms waiting for you to conquer.

Remember, no matter how noble your aims are, you are not Hercules. You will not be granted residence on Mount Olympus and be elevated to the status of a 'demi-god.'

Then what journey should you embark upon? What is the real-life equivalent of these stories and tales? How will you know what the true purpose of your life is?

Well, to answer this, you must revisit history because since the advent of humankind, probably every human has tried to define the purpose of his existence.

You are no different!

So, let's take a look at history and see how different societies have constructed their value systems, systems that helped people develop a clear vision for their lives.

Ancient philosophy and the meaning of life

Take a look at Socrates and his idea of cultivating *Eudaimonia*, i.e., continuous betterment to live a good life. One of his most admired statements is that "The unexamined life is not worth living."

If you ever had the fortune to read the Platonic dialogues, you will realize that the philosopher urges people and society to constantly contemplate the world around them.

So, if you only reflect on yourself and save a little time to introspect, you will reach a better understanding of yourself and your desires. Once you can connect with your innermost self, you can make conscious choices that align with your values and beliefs.

Socrates deemed it essential to challenge existing values and beliefs to ensure that the human race could grow into their better selves.

If you don't question, then there is a chance that you will remain stagnant, not allowing yourself the opportunity to reach deeper into understanding the meaning behind the ideals that define who you are.

In ancient societies, people maintained certain moral or religious principles and believed that to be the purpose of their lives. They spent years trying to become the best at what they thought was their role, i.e., a father, mother, neighbor, warrior, merchant, or a farmer, etc. The social roles assigned to them through their lives defined their sense of purpose. From building families or nurturing communal bonds, they remained stuck in fulfilling their familial and societal roles.

Additionally, the guiding light for most societies back then was religion and their beliefs in God.

However, in modern times, the influence of religion has decreased for most people. Plus, you do not have to dedicate your entire day to farming your food or protecting your lands and yourselves from imminent danger.

That means you now have the time, energy, and resources to enrich your life with greater meaning.

All you have to do is sustain your lives by earning a suitable income. Then, you have the privilege to live life on your terms. You have the liberty to choose your career path, place of residence, your plans of travel, and objects of your monetary expenditure. You can pursue your dreams and have a lot more freedom and resources than a man who lived in ancient Egypt or Native America.

The world has changed so drastically in the last few centuries. Now more than ever, the question *'what is the purpose of life?'* has become quite relevant.

How can you answer this question? Why should you answer this question?

Throughout countless works of philosophers, you will encounter their attempts at outlining the values that ought to dictate your choices. As humans, you are consistently striving towards a life that can be deemed as worth living. But what should be the driving force behind your actions to transform into your better selves?

The short answer is "focus.". You must be focused on what brings you sublime joy.

Staying focused on your goals and ambitions will propel you *forward*. It should be the inner state of your mind, soul, and body. It allows you to live your life with a passion rather than just fulfilling an obligation.

The focus will not come naturally to you, and you will find it hard to stay motivated all the time. Sometimes, you may feel like not doing anything.

On such days, it is imperative to slow down and ask yourself, *'what's wrong?'*

Maybe you are experiencing some profound level of inner conflict that is causing a disruption. For you to remain focused, you should firmly believe in what is said next.

A genuine passion to be successful stems from self-acceptance and self-love.

Let's explore how and why.

What's your unique sense of purpose?

Remember in first grade when your homeroom teachers asked you to write on a piece of paper what you wanted to be when you grew up. What did you write?

When you were young, everything you knew was limited – all you had ever known of the world came from a couple of storybooks, cartoons, or your parents. How do you think you might have answered back then? You might have aspired to become a doctor, astronaut, scientist, or maybe a teacher.

As the kid in you grew up, you learned about more professions and your likes and dislikes. And till your adolescence, your ideas must have kept on changing, and there is still a slim chance that even today, you are uncertain whether becoming a project manager was the right choice. You were a starry-eyed kid once, and as you grew up, you must have had different sets of dreams, hopes, aspirations, and ideals.

But while you grew up, without realizing it, you had started a journey just like the young Hercules did. It might not be as heroic or grand, but it was a journey nonetheless, one that will cease only with your death.

When it comes to feeling motivated, start with constantly questioning your ideas and motives. You will notice the subtle yet powerful effects of questioning yourself on your life.

Often, people end up choosing completely different paths in their lives than they initially planned. You might have worked very hard in life to be an accountant or an H.R. executive, but it is entirely possible that as you grew up, you decided to become a project manager, a team leader, and an influencer. One day you might have realized that your earlier dreams didn't bring you the sense of fulfillment you crave in life. At that very thought, you must sit down and contemplate. What has changed? Why has it changed? Why do you suddenly feel inclined to pursue a career in project management or Information Technology? Or why suddenly do you feel tempted to become a freelancer and traverse the world at your will. It is equally possible that you feel a definite shift in your priorities from wanting to build a successful career to wanting to become a nomadic traveler.

If you ever find yourself a little lost and unable to know what you want, then embrace that moment as a chance for growth.

Self-acceptance and communication are key!

Something is changing in your mind. Let the change come organically. You need to foster a healthy mental environment for the change to take seed in your mind and bloom. Treat yourself with care instead of frustration, even though you might be tempted to disregard your anxieties as not worthwhile. Remember that people are constantly changing and growing. Your mind is growing with time, too, and it will go through awkward growth spurts just like your physical body once did. Instead of condemning yourself for undergoing a 'weird' phase, try to be open to change.

Don't hesitate to introspect

Try to sit down with yourself after every little while and understand why you are changing. Try to connect with your emotions.

Once you are honest with yourself, you will understand what you believe is your purpose in life. Once you identify it, you will know that it is your ultimate life force.

Your desperation to fulfill your life goals is what will drive you forward in life. If you plan your life consciously, one day, you will look back and be content with the course you took in life.

Life offers unique opportunities to everyone. Everyone will boast of different life experiences that paved their path and made them who they are.

Throughout life, you will find yourselves at the point where you will wonder, "Why am I living?"

"What do I want to live for? What do I envision for myself?"

"When I look back, will I be content with the life I have led, or will regrets swarm me?"

The most straightforward answer to these questions is that there is no singular purpose in your life. As you grow and your outlook of the world grows, your purpose in life will evolve, and so will your answer to these questions. As for regrets, here is an essential lesson for you as a project manager:

Do not waste your time regretting what your values do to your past.

At one point, it was your present, and you had made the best choices you could with the wisdom and knowledge you had back then. Yes, when you look back, you may think you should have done things differently, but do not berate yourself for how life served you your cards. Just remind yourself, you played the best trick with the choices and limited outlook you had.

Like the tides that ebb and flow at the seashore, your perception of life and purpose too will be in constant flux. Even when you think you have finally found your calling, you might find yourself at crossroads again. Do not despair: stop, breathe and reflect again on your course of life.

Use self-communication tools

One such tool is *Ikigai*. If you have ever read a self-help book about getting successful or heard wellness coaches speak, you might be familiar with the Japanese term *Ikigai*.

The concept rose to popularity in the 1800s and was centered on promoting the state of wellbeing in people. The idea advocates that you should pursue things that lay at the center of what you love, what you are good at, what the world needs, and what you can be paid for. It is a way of life and an approach that impacts every choice people make. If you ensure that this logic dictates your choices, then it is believed that you will live a meaningful life. Some people even believe that practicing *Ikigai* is the secret behind the long-life spans of the Japanese people.

There are other ways to stay emotionally grounded and self-aware. From journaling to taking up swimming, there is a lot you can do to start giving yourself the mental space to understand yourself.

If you talk to a writer who has to create compelling stories as a profession, they will tell you to start journaling regularly. Start penning down your thoughts on the paper. It does not have to make sense. What you write is for your eyes only. There is no pressure to say the right things. Just take out the scrambled mess of your thoughts. After every little while, you can choose to revisit your thoughts.

You will quickly decipher what thoughts, including general concerns, hopes, anxieties, insecurities, or goals, plague your mind. You can take that moment to reflect on what that says about who you are becoming or want to become. More than anything, you will be able to understand yourself better.

Even though you have spent the entirety of your life with yourself, as you reflect on your thoughts, you may realize that until then, you had practically been a stranger to yourself.

Treat yourself with the same consideration, respect, and effort as you would treat any family member or a friend.

Self-discovery is a constant factor that will elevate your living experience.

You must always endeavor to discover and rediscover yourself. Once you know about your changing expectations from life, only then can you lead a successful life.

What does a 'purpose in life' look like?

Everyone has a different purpose in life. No matter if it looks similar on the surface, your drive and perceptions will differ drastically from even your siblings, even when you have the same goal. Recognize your passion and your individual calling.

Can your purpose in life be that you want to become rich and accomplished? Yes.

Can your purpose in life be that you want to be remembered as a force of good in other people's lives? Yes.

Can your purpose in life be that you want to experience self-fulfillment and explore the world? Yes.

Can you have a purpose in life that's all of the above? Yes.

Everyone's *raison d'être* will look different. It might be about following a specific set of values or collecting tangible assets, or both.

All you have to do is to know what gives you joy. In your journey of becoming a successful person, all you need to know is what sparks happiness for you.

Live life on your terms; You must have heard this statement quite often – this assertion that's supposed to be an encouragement to live life without any shackles. But most people do not even *know* what their terms are. How will you live your truth when you have never discovered it?

If you have learned anything in the last few pages, now you must be asking yourself, "what value did this chapter add to my life? How can it help me in my journey of becoming a good project manager?"

If you asked this question, kudos! You have begun on the journey to self-discovery.

Why is self-discovery important? As a project manager, you are the leader of your team. You must inspire and motivate them, but it will never be possible if you are wishy-washy about your own life goals and aims. How can you guide your team to reach their true potential when every day you are plagued with thoughts that make you doubt yourself and your potential?

Secondly, when you are self-aware, only then can you help your team be self-aware. As you will read on, you will discover the importance of having a "vision" and a "shared vision." However, having a vision brings you back to the first stepping stone: knowing what you want from life, from your career, and from your job. Once you answer that, you can go on struggling towards a destination. Without it, you are bound to get stranded.

Defining Your Vision

Simply continue the process of questioning yourself. As the French saying goes, we are all born with a raison d'être - the reason for our existence. Our job is to find out what it is.

It is easy to get lost in the comfort of short-term achievements, which act as rewards when we fulfill them. Did you want to buy a car or learn an instrument? How did you feel when you drove the car through the garage or when you finally learned to play a song on the instrument?

Once you get what you want, you will feel accomplished, which will make you want to do better. But once you get out of the haze of short-term achievements, you begin to see that all of these little acts add to the larger vision of who you want to be.

The closer you get to that vision, the more gratification you will feel. This feedback loop of satisfaction fuels your focus. It is only possible to keep this loop going if your actions are consistent with what you believe is your life's purpose.

If you have finally answered your questions in life, it's the right time to find clarity in your vision.

Imagine a project manager preaching technical concepts and setting assumptions and risks on project tasks while they themselves are not aligned with their passions.

So be focused in your life, and then once you have done your grinding, define your vision and then live it in reality, nurture it and inspire others. Others include everyone who's related to you: your subordinates, your family, and your colleagues.

So, ask yourself, what is your vision? What type of vision will help you get closer to success? What does growth look like to you? What do you envision for yourself in your professional and personal life? Do you want to see yourself as a leader?

Everyone has a vision, perhaps a picture of what they want to be. A vision is the bigger picture of how things should be in the future. Imagine a billboard image of where you want to be in the future. Do you see yourself working towards it?

Every day as you go about your life, you may find yourself thinking about how you can be better at what you do. But do you ever strive for the answer? Most probably not! Because really, have you ever tried to identify the gap between who you are now and who you want to be?

Let's look at what Sakichi Toyoda, Toyota's founder, had to say about this. According to him, you need first to clarify the problem with your own eyes to move forward in the process. So, you need first to visualize the "Gap" between your current and future state.

If, as a project manager, you are rigorously self-aware of your current state, future state, and the things you need to get to your future state, you will achieve success.

Ask yourself, who is the future you? What do you want from life?

You will have a list of things that you would want from your life, and once you enlist them, you might top it off by saying your vision is to be "a successful Project Manager" or maybe "A successful Project manager with an undeniable legacy."

Remember, the difference might be subtle, but your vision will define your direction and purpose of life and your future aspirations. And this vision will underpin your strategy to your work and will also link your stakeholders to it. You must announce your vision to all the people who can contribute valuable expertise to achieving your goal. Some people may skip this step, but they will lose precious pieces of advice and priceless wisdom. You would need to invest double the time to realize your ambition because you never brought anyone on board to paddle you closer to your destiny.

Have you ever broken down the problems that made your real-life hitch? So, breathe and do it now and give yourself a chance to identify and see which problem out of all your problems is actually hindering your progress. You might instantly want to remove all your obstacles from your life, but you always start from things that you can control first. You can have an extensive laundry list of problems that you want to resolve, but it all comes down to having enough time, resources and prioritizing the one that you can start with, and once you have fixed it, you can always go back and resolve others too. A simple suggestion here is to list all your problems and pick the important one (define your urgency yourself). Remember, Kaizen (improvement) only comes when you have clarity in your visions and values. Work on clarifying your values and keep evolving into your future self.

Importance of Shared Vision

Once you have a clear vision, you are only halfway to your goal. When working in a team, you must also have a "shared vision." This vision must include a shared understanding of material aims, preferred working environment, and ambitions with everyone working on the project to make it into reality.

Let's look into the necessity for a shared vision and how it may be achieved.

Ben was a visionary Project Manager, and like you, he realized the necessity for a shared vision, and he wanted to impart the same lesson to his team.

Thus, he gathered them for a meeting on a warm, sunny day. He wanted them to have a clear head for the session ahead because he believed unless his team converged on a shared vision, they couldn't make progress.

Ben, with his seven years of experience in heading project teams, called the gathered team members to attention, "All right, Good morning, everyone."

There were inaudible whispers and disinterested nods, and he knew he was right to call this meeting now.

"You all have 5 minutes to gather up and join me here (pointing towards the space in the corner near the whiteboard)" he took the marker from the table and continued, "We have been talking about the importance of having a shared vision as a team. Today, I will try to show what might happen if we don't clarify what we want as a team. That also includes not knowing how to act motivated as a team."

He placed a chair in front of him.

"Let's pretend that this (pointing to the black chair) is a hill covered with snow, and you have to reach the red flag downhill, 3 miles from here. Now, suppose John and Sara," he pointed to the two project developers on the team, "have to sled downhill. They have only one sled between them, and they have no choice but to ride double. Halfway down, they got into a jutting rock, and the sled broke. They try to fix it, but they can't. Suddenly they saw two project engineers from the project team coming over the hill."

Ben called Leo and Mary forward as the project engineers. The rest of the team members were asked to observe. Then Ben presented the disharmony in vision.

Ben claimed, "Now Sarah thinks they should stop the engineers and ask for help. John disagrees. He believes there is no use wasting time and asking for help. Instead, they should just start trekking towards the flag. Could the participants please start the roleplay and see what kind of a team we have at hand. Remember, you four are single teams, and you must reach the red flag at 10. It is already 9 PM.

Sarah and John begin the act where the sled broke.

Sarah (developer): Oh, I'm sorry, John. The sled has broken, and now none of us will be able to reach the flag in time.

John (developer): No, never mind! It was an old sled and was meant to break.

Sarah (developer): But I think I might be able to fix it, or I can wait for the project engineers to come and help. They might be able to fix it. I can't do it alone.

John (developer): Well, you can try, but I don't think those engineers would even stop to help; they won't do anything.

Sarah (developer): Maybe you are right, but I will still try my luck. After all, I don't have any tools, and we have to make it to the top of the hill together before 10:00 PM.

John (developer) (to Leo and Mary) Will you help us fix our sled?

Leo (Engineer): Well, this appears to be an old unmaintained sled. I don't want to waste time fixing something that has no hope. It's already close to 9. I must reach the flag in time. Then I can send a rescue team for you.

John to Sarah: isn't this what I told you!

Mary: But Leo, I have an idea. Surely, we four can drag the sled to the small hut you can see there. I am sure somebody there can help with the repair.

Sarah: Thank you, Mary! That's a brilliant idea!

Leo reluctantly agrees, and John is chafed at being proven wrong.

At this point, Ben clapped his hands and called a stop. "Thank you, everyone. You four did a good job; please take your seats.

Now I want the observers to share their feedback.

He constructed a chart on the whiteboard and asked the observer, "What do you think was lacking in Leo?

- Observer 1 said: empathy
- Observer 2 said: team spirit
- Observer 3 said: Compassion

Observer 4 said: I think he was working for his personal goals and not for the team.

Ben asked, and what was lacking in John?

- Observer 1 said: Trust
- Observer 2 said: yes, he didn't trust his team!
- Observer 3 said: I think he doesn't know how to work in a team.

Ben drew a chart on the board and wrote the heading "Teamwork is everything," and with it comes success. And to have a shared vision, your core values should be

- Trust
- Responsibility
- Teamwork
- Empathy

Ben turned his face towards his team and said, "I put you in this dramatic situation to set you in a stage of conflict so that you can objectively see the behaviors and their effect on the team at large. I hope I was able to clarify the importance of "having similar values and vision." Remember, if you all don't think that helping and making a collaborative effort is essential, then you will never be able to achieve success together.

Then Bill asked, "what saved the team?"

John: Mary's effort to go the extra mile! She was able to provide a solution that everyone could agree on.

Bill nodded and smiled. "You hit the bull's eye, John. Did you all see what Mary did? May you have all the right traits to be a project leader. You were able to unite them for a shared goal. Even if Leo had reached the red flag on time, the team would have lost. A good team must work together."

He continued, "So the big questions that you need to ask to establish an understanding of your vision are: What impact do you want to make at work? Where do you want to see yourself in the next five years? Once you can answer these questions, I am sure we will all be following a single map and working towards one single goal between our present and future."

"So, establishing a vision is not just for your project or company growth only. It will help you in achieving your success, your dreams, and your passions." Ben concluded.

Whether you start a company, construction, research, or an I.T. project, the first step is to set your vision, and the second step is to have the right "people" who are committed and aligned with that vision.

What differentiates a company that's successful from a company that's struggling? It shouldn't take a genius to reply that it comes with a dedicated and passionate 'workforce.'

You might not know how to succeed in your project implementation, but you should know that the right people in the right roles with the right vision will promise success. So, begin with "who" should be the people rather than finding the "what" when trying to devise your project vision for your long-term success.

Secondly, if you have the right self-motivated and disciplined team, you won't have to work hard around them as much as you will have to if you had the wrong people on board. Right people in the right roles will cut your workload by half. Be warned! Always cleanse the wrong people off your project and then start.

You will see that the right people will naturally blend, inspire, engage and lead other people in the process. They will catalyze your project to the heights you imagined for it.

Set Values and Goals

Goals

You may be eager to know the technicalities of becoming a project manager. Still, you will realize the importance of "vision, values and goals" when you practice meditation in your life and see the improved version of yourself, the person who will not only say things but actually do it.

Who do you think is better? A Project manager who just plans or the manager who actually walks the walk and talks the talk.

You will study the details of Project Management essentials in chapter 4, and from there, you will accelerate fast on your path to your project's success.

However, before delving into actual "project management," you must first explore your core values and know about your own goals. This will help you in defining you, your management, and your relation with your team forever.

So, question yourself repeatedly

"What is the real purpose of my life?"

Is it a common, universal purpose? Are humans inherently engineered to have a purpose in life? Will not having a purpose in life make you feel lost?

You're likely in a headspace where you're trying to understand how to become a better version of yourself. However, these are heavy, abstract questions that one can go on for days trying to explain and need years' worth of lived experience to come up with a "right answer."

The path to self-improvement is often littered with the opinions and experiences of others, of things they have seen, and stories they have to tell. Can those work for you? Absolutely. But should you wholly depend on another's lived experience to define and design yours? Absolutely not! Doing so will be a recipe for disaster. All humans exist within geographically and psychologically set boundaries, with thoughts and opinions differing from each other. Of course, that doesn't mean all, but a certain percentage of your thoughts are likely different from even the closest friend you have. And yet, you coexist with them beautifully.

Similarly, when it comes to motivational speakers, you must listen to them with keen ears. Their stories and experiences are exciting to hear, mainly because they have a knack for storytelling. Still, they cannot be imposed on everyone, especially your personal life.

You are a different human being who has lived through varying experiences, and you have your unique situation. You should not feel pressured to follow someone else's life path.

However, that doesn't mean you shouldn't listen to successful people; they can be a great source of motivation to achieve goals. They excite you; they inspire you, and they help you find better solutions to your problems. The key, however, is to take their advice with a grain of salt.

It is common knowledge that setting goals is essential, but you might not realize how important it is as you continue to move through life. Setting goals helps trigger new behaviors, guides your focus, and enables you to sustain momentum in life. Successful people in business, athletes, and high achievers in their fields all set goals. But there is an art to setting goals. As Confucius put it, "When it becomes obvious that the goals cannot be reached, don't adjust the goals, adjust the action steps." You have already achieved a goal halfway if you have set it. More often than not, setting an intention to fulfill a dream can motivate you to complete it.

When you set sharp and clearly defined goals, it gives you long-term vision and short-term motivation. You become more disciplined as a person as it helps you organize your time and your resources so that you know what you need to achieve a goal. This works exceptionally well for short-term goals. But what is most important when setting goals is understanding the goal priority. You're going to want to achieve multiple goals at once, and not all have to have a significant impact. Still, whatever the goals are, if you go about achieving them haphazardly, chances are you're not going to feel satisfied or excited about achieving a goal as much.

So, while you're setting your goals, you need to prioritize what you want to achieve and time it in a certain way. Thus, in a roundabout way, goal setting ends up teaching you to discipline yourself.

Path to Setting Personal Goals

Setting goals is a process that changes over time. What you wanted to achieve in your twenties might not matter as much anymore. Your motivation to achieve a specific goal might not drive your sense of discipline any longer. However, this isn't restricted to your age; instead, any change in the situation can lead to different life goals.

You go through several levels while setting your goals, starting with creating a bigger picture of what you want to do with your life. That means how do you see yourself in 10 years? When you have a vague idea of what you want, that can help identify the goals you will achieve. Then you can break those down into smaller and smaller targets that you can hit to reach your lifetime goals. And once you're done setting these goals, the next step is to achieve them.

Setting Lifetime Goals

The first step to achieving any goal is considering what you want to do in your lifetime. This is not limited to just your career or family; rather, it gives a broad coverage of all essential areas in your life. What level do you want to reach in your career? Do you plan to move from your job? Are there smaller goals that you have decided for your learning during this job? Are you family-oriented? If you're thinking of becoming a parent, how do you want to bring up your children?

You're going to have to spend some time brainstorming these questions or any relevant to your situation and goals. Just remember whatever goals you want to achieve; they need to be realistic and genuine. Your motivation to achieve a goal is intrinsically connected to how much you want to achieve it. For example, if you have to make decisions because family and friends influence you, you might not be motivated to complete the goal. You can consider what they want, but the key is to stay true to yourself.

Set Smaller Goals

Lifetime goals lead the way to smaller goals. Think of this as a five-year plan of smaller goals. This gives you a deadline for completion and adds to your life plans. But you can also break these plans down to one-year or six-month plans, depending on what is your priority and what is easily achievable.

To-do lists are a great way to ensure you stay with the deadline and have a vision for what your months or days can look like. However, remember not to overwhelm yourself with too many goals. Often that can result in losing motivation to achieve these goals regardless of how much you want to.

Sometimes goals as simple as completing a book can give you a sense of accomplishment. That feeling works wonders in motivating you. Plus, as you feel a sense of happiness at having achieved something, you're likely going to see improvement in the quality and realism of your goal setting.

According to a published paper for "A Theory of Goal Setting & Task Performance" by Locke and Latham, there are five goal-setting principles that can help improve your chances of success.

1- Clarity is a great motivator when it comes to setting goals. When you're specific and clear about your goals, it eliminates any chances of confusion, so you do not have to figure out what to do next or behind your lifetime goals.

2- Commitment to your goals is important. If you're not committed to a goal, you'll find it hard to achieve it.

3- Challenging goals can excite the human brain and expand your horizon. Such goals keep you on your toes and make you learn important life lessons, pushing you to achieve more challenging goals in life.

4- Feedback from your peers or family members is a great way to gauge whether you're doing the right thing and how you're doing it. Plus, you can adjust your expectations accordingly and create a plan of action moving forward.

5- Task complexing means having goals that are aligned with how complex your goals are. This keeps you in check with the reality of achieving that goal.

When you have achieved a goal, take the time to enjoy the satisfaction of having done so.

Goals and Success

Goals are closely linked to motivation. Setting a goal is a powerful way to keep you focused, feeling productive, and improve your determination to work. Success thrives on the need to gain recognition and praise from others or yourself. For example, if you had been working towards getting a promotion and you've achieved that milestone at work, you're going to feel more motivated at work and excited for your job.

Plus, you'll likely care more about committing yourself to a job if you've previously seen positive results of a goal you achieved. Similarly, incentivizing your goals can also give you that added motivation to see yourself through goal completion.

For example, if you want a raise, think of a higher standard of living you can acquire with the extra pay, and that might excite you or energize you to achieve your sales quota, etc., for the raise.

Once you have your goals set, you can also use them as tools for success. Keep in mind that as much as outside factors impact your motivation levels and can boost them for a short period, what keeps you consistently focused is how you view your goals and self-conversations. If you're feeling weighed down by an assignment, think of positive outcomes after completion. Imagine that you will have free time to concentrate on other things, plus the anxiety of having to complete this task will go away. Imagine how proud you will feel after you get your result and how enjoyable it will be to share your happiness with others on it

For many, happiness, contentment, satisfaction, and, to a great extent, living a comfortable life are universally acknowledged goals. These are what a person is consistently trying to achieve throughout their complete course of life. Of course, this does not make them unattainable; instead, as we grow older, our wants and needs change accordingly. Eventually, what brought you happiness a few years ago might not hold the same place in your life anymore.

Having goals for things you want to do and working towards them is essential for being human. Be it something as simple as having breakfast every morning before you leave for work. It is that little something you do for your physical wellbeing that adds to the ultimate goal, i.e., happiness. However, the path towards achieving a plan might not always run smoothly; you will encounter untoward situations and learn lessons. But the key to what makes life good is accepting what is and moving forward with what you have.

The human brain is used to structure and discipline in life. More often than not, having a routine you follow, an ideology you identify with, or values that reflect your personality add a sense of meaning and purpose, pointing you in the direction you want to go in life.

What Are Your Values?

Everyone has a vague idea of what values they believe in. You might not know what your core values are, but that's alright. You can start figuring out what values you believe in with some time and self-reflection.

But first, let's think about what having 'values' means?

A simple definition of values is a set of ideas or beliefs that influence your choices, actions, and thoughts. That's why they play a central role in shaping who you are. Your values could be anything between honesty, generosity, kindness, practicality, loyalty, excellence, pursuing happiness, success, and more. What values do you believe in more?

Imagine.

You got an unexpected bonus from your job. What do you do with it? Do you buy presents for your loved ones? Do you add the money to your travel fund? Do you donate the money to a charity or help out someone in need? Or do you add it to your savings account?

Your loved one is going through an emotionally difficult period. At work, you have some projects that you need to work on. Do you try to finish your work, or do you take time off work to be there for your loved one? Do you try to pull in a favor from a colleague and delegate your tasks someplace?

You are planning to buy groceries for the month but are low on budget. Do you buy just the essentials? Do you borrow some money from a close friend to buy everything you need to live comfortably?

There are various scenarios you can think of to figure out your core values.

How do you determine your core values?

To determine the core values that are important to you, start listing down 5-7 core values that appeal to you the most. This activity is often used by personal development coaches and is enormously helpful. If you are at a loss and can't think of what values you believe in, then start thinking about the people you admire or respect. Think about the person you grew up admiring, even if it is a fictional character from a cartoon or a movie. Ask yourself what characteristics of this person made an impression on you.

For example, you might have grown up idolizing someone like Mother Teresa, known for her compassion and service towards the underprivileged. Think about Florence Nightingale, the British nurse who showed great dedication and empathy in supporting those who needed medical care. You can have great respect for historical leaders like Washington or Abraham Lincoln for their forthrightness and intelligence. The passion of such people is awe-inspiring and can leave a strong impact on you. But these are historical figures. You might have great admiration for people in your family, maybe one of your parents, grandparents, aunts, or uncles. If there are specific characteristics that you want to emulate, then you can add them to your list of values.

Try thinking about your happiest and saddest memories to get to the bottom of what values are most important to you. Recall those memories and focus on your feelings.

Here is a scenario.

Josh is a young medical student and is enjoying a casual dinner with his friends. His friends are sharing stories about what inspired them to get into the grueling medical profession. When Josh is asked to share his story, he thinks back to his childhood when his grandparents were sick and unable to find proper care in their locality and city.

He sat on the table, thinking for a moment, and then replied, "I wanted to become a doctor or a nurse to help treat people. But I want to become a good doctor – someone who is sincere to his patients and profession. I don't want to just cash money from my job."

For Josh, his goal is to become a doctor, but his values are kindness for the ill and sincerity to his position.

This is just one example to understand how values work in conjunction with your goals.

Remember,

"Setting your goals and values is not an easy process. It can take you a day, or it can take you multiple months of pondering – it's different for everyone. The sooner you get started, the better it will be for you! The earlier you begin, the sooner you will reach self-awareness.

CHAPTER FOUR

ESSENTIALS

Enter Caption

Bennie Johnson was a project manager with a hands-on engineering background. In Jan 2019, after five years of sabbatical, he was offered a job as a project manager in industrial processes in France. The job was heavily process-driven with the delivery of goods, auto parts, and services. At the onset, he was expected to produce results with no prior orientation and training. Few months after his joining, Bennie started working on a multi-million-euro contract. He had a rocky start, but as the dust settled, he started getting the hang of things.

During the project, Bennie realized that his core strengths were conflict and risk management, and he was also excellent at keeping his clients happy. For Bennie, it was mainly about focusing on clients' needs and not about following the process perfect to the T.

Soon after his mega project completion, he started engaging in smaller projects. One such project with X.Y.Z. Company didn't come to closure as expected. He recalls it as a "disaster."

Bennie started, *"It was a Wednesday afternoon; I went to pay a visit to my client's office on 16th avenue and was given a tour by one of the salesmen of the old industrial building. The spare-part room was being refurbished, and there was a lot of noise inside, so I got out quickly. I was waiting at the door when I saw a man with a black-tie walking towards me. I believe he was one of the customer representative staff. He called out, "Hello, Sir! I am Eric. Please follow me."*

I started marching behind him, with my leather bag at my side. We passed the visitors lounge, and I saw some men sitting down on a bench waiting. Some office men were on break, and some were waiting for the delivery notes to be signed.

I asked, "Eric, are we going to get Mr. Jerry to speak with me today? He seems to be a busy man."

"Yes, Yes, please go inside," he replied as he waved me into the meeting room.

I walked towards the General Manager who was looking rather busy with his documents,

"Bennie, please take a seat," said Mr. Jerry gesturing me to sit while he took a seat behind his desk. "Mr. Jerry, I understand you require a new certificate before closure, but I wanted to be sure that you are ready to bear the charges," I spoke

"Yes, Bennie, I understand, and I am open to paying for the compensation," he replied

"That's great," I replied.

After getting my concern across, I discussed with him his business affairs for a few minutes. He was pretty eager about how he was investing in infrastructure to make it a successful manufacturing unit. A few minutes later, he got up and said he had to leave for somewhere. I thanked him for his time and left. As I drove back to my office, I wondered how I would get the certificate made. When I reached the office, I called almost everyone in the department who I thought would be able to help me, but almost everyone turned a cold shoulder. Some said they didn't have the time, and some outright refused, saying, "You should know the process. Please don't bother us again."

Bennie says, "I managed to complete my task, but I had to amend the purchase order to charge the client, and again for that, I was met with hostile responses, "Where is the documentation, Bennie? This is incomplete! This is not the process."

"Of course, it's not the process, but I believe that once in a while, a little change in the process to keep the client happy should bring no harm," Bennie muttered.

But the day ended in running here and there. Moreover, the project closure wasn't a straightforward one. Two days later, Bennie's team member came running to him, saying, "Sir! Mr. Jerry is not responding for the next order we talked about!"

Bennie knew he had lost his client because the people were not ready to accept the change. The company lost a potential two-year contract valuing a million euros. Most of all, a relatively happy client got disgruntled because of the delay caused in meeting his needs.

Bennie also realized that his approach needed some corrections. He realized that processes couldn't be skipped entirely, and people needed to support the process rather than putting hurdles along the way. He also admitted that keeping good relationships with the internal stakeholder was equally important as keeping the clients happy. His success in the company would not be possible if he kept ignoring the people and the processes. He figured out the equation correctly in his mind now.

People + Process = Success and Innovation

He realized with people and process comes innovation, and with innovation comes success.

As a project manager, you need to remember that people and processes are both significant. When you start managing the process, you will have to have good relationships at work to see your processes flourish.

Remember, you cannot enforce project management techniques and methods if you fail to empower and train your people. People can work for and against you in this process, and to achieve long-term success, you will have to first be the role model, follow what you preach, and inspire your team to take ownership while committing to the process from the beginning to the end.

So, can you really control people by coaxing them all the time?

Or can you force your team to work better?

The answer is No. Your role is tested every step of the way. And let's not forget, as a project manager, you have to get work done from people who are not even in your team. Sometimes people don't even report to you. So, what do you do about that? You can't essentially order them to perform. What you need to do is to make connections with people at large, understand them and be someone who is liked and respected. Again, the authority will come with your actions.

The Second Project Bennie Johnson got was better than the last one. He made the WBS structure well, and although the project met some changes on the course, they all were met smoothly. He followed the process and was on better terms with the team now. He structured everything well according to the formula, and he found his way out even on close calls.

And he never realized that not following the SAP request for procurement and being late in following project schedules had always hurt his position.

The same project coordinator who used to think Bennie could never be a good Project Manager now trusted him with his tasks. Of course, Beanie had turned a new page. He worked hard on keeping good relations with those around him. No wonder his growth and success were tenfold.

He didn't quit despite all his frustrations and over-sensitivity. He made it when most didn't.

He learnt that by practicing processes and people management skills, he could manipulate his ways to get the output he desired. He was even able to pull extensions and extra favors with the otherwise pragmatic and stiff clients. He also learned that asking questions from his team and solving their problems helped keep him connected to them on multiple levels.

What did you learn from Bennie? Did you see the importance of people and processes in ensuring success as a project manager?

Being a project manager is not an aloof position. A project manager is closely tied to the team, accountable to the stakeholders, bound by processes, and burdened by the provided environment. A project manager can never flourish unless they adapt to these three factors. They can never act independently of these domains. While people and processes have always been important for a project manager, in recent years, there has been a new domain that a project manager must tackle: the domain of environment, especially a rapidly evolving one.

People + Processes + Environment = Successful Project Manager.

While you may be concerned with delivering a successful project, it is unlikely that you would not be invested in seeing your personal growth. A project manager must learn to work in these three domains if he wants to be successful.

It is upon you how you use these three domains to your advantage! They can be your hurdles in delivering a top-notch project, or they could be your weapon and strength.

Let's look closely at each of these domains and how they can either trip you up or take you higher.

Domain I: People

Christopher was proud to be a project manager. He thought his position gave him the highest authority. He also had a diploma certificate in Project Management. When he first graduated from university, he got job opportunities from five leading firms, and obviously, he chose the most well-paid and reputable one.

This company already had three other project teams and project managers. But the other P.M.s all lacked professional training for being a project manager since it was relatively a new discipline. Christopher had an edge. These project managers had spent years learning their role, but Christopher already had the essential knowledge to accelerate his start. He also had the benefit of choosing and employing his team. He hired fresh graduates like himself.

"They will all bring a fresh perspective and innovative ideas. They will also learn to respect authority. If I bring someone more experienced than myself, I will have to teach them to respect me and follow my lead," Christopher justified to himself as he built up his team.

On his first project, during the project initiation, he quickly brought all the stakeholders on board. He also got the budget approved in no time. He had no major trouble in coming this far.

There were just minor inconveniences. The accounts manager thought that the budget was minimal, and Christopher had not kept a margin for risk aversion. Christopher was sure there were no significant risks in sight, and increasing the budget any further would require him to coax the shareholder unnecessarily.

Maggie, another team member, said that they had failed to account for a significant stakeholder. Since the project concerned the upgradation of a public center, she insisted that the locals should also have a say. Christopher ended the objection by saying, "Obviously, their welfare has been well thought of. The community chair hires us, and sure he is a fair representation of all."

Christopher knew that to be a project manager, he must be strong-headed, or else his team would never meet deadlines, so he was doing just that!

Do you see anything wrong with that?

Christopher might have employed the most talented team, but he did not take their expertise seriously. He was an autocratic leader, and that could put him in definite trouble.

Can you list down the troubles he may have invited upon himself?

1. He ignored the advice of the accountant.

2. He ignored Maggie's advice without further study.

3. He did miss an essential stakeholder for the project.

Do you want to know what happened next?

The public did get furious at not being involved in the planning process. They demanded a proper demonstration of the project planning. Ultimately, Christopher had to organize a big council meeting – an unexpected addition to the project cost. The locals insisted that the project should also include a small playhouse for kids. This, too, was an addition to the project cost. Now, Cristopher had to revise the entire budget and bring the stakeholders on board again. His team was not very happy with him. They thought all this mess could have been avoided if Christopher had heard them and valued their opinion from the beginning.

Do you know the most significant error Christopher had made?

He failed to work along with the people in his domain. Can you recognize the people a project manager must learn to deal with?

1. Stakeholders

2. The project team

3. The dealers/contractors

This looks like a lot of work. All these people enjoy a unique relationship with the project manager and must be treated differently. The stakeholders have a significant say about the project when it begins. They will also be interested in the last deliverables. All the stakeholders will have varying and, at times, conflicting interests in the project. A successful project manager must learn to keep all his stakeholders happy to avoid bumps in the project. This may seem like a daunting task, but here is a helpful tip.

Start by recognizing the essential shareholder first, the one who has the highest bearing on the operation. Then work downwards. This way, you can prioritize the demands of the important shareholder and negotiate with the smaller fish.

Then comes the team members. The team members are like the wheels of a gear. They all have different aptitudes and different functions. They also have different personalities. A project manager must make them all work together in harmony towards a "shared vision." Not everyone on the team will have the group spirit. Not all will be as dedicated to the project as you. Now you must showcase your skill as a leader. You want them all to march to your beat.

Likewise, not every member on your team will be qualified to embark on the project on the first call of "go." Some may require additional training and that too falls in your job description. You must arrange additional training sessions for them. You are responsible for how your team performs and if your team lags. Their failures and triumphs will all be directed towards you.

Lastly, during the project, you may also be involved in buying and selling. This also falls in the people's domains. You must maintain cordial ties with these people too. You must also maintain complete records for all your dealings. This brings you to your next domain: the processes domain.

Domain II: Process

In the process domain, the Project Manager needs to have a rich skill portfolio. This domain needs you to acquire some functional and technical skills for performing the work of a project manager. You will have to know the business concepts and processes. You will also have to understand the business expectations and then analyze the capabilities of your project team. You must execute your projects smartly to deliver business value to all the involved stakeholders. You must also develop an approach for things like:

- Communications to risk management
- Budget and resource management
- Schedule to Quality management

- Scope to project change management
- Procurement to configuration management

You will study the steps of the project management life cycle in the last chapter, and the above point will be dealt with in detail in the Execution Phase.

So as a leader of their entire team, it would be best if you overlooked a range of operations and processes. Imagine a project team. There will ideally be an accountant, a risk analyst, a communication in-charge, and a resource allocator. You may also recall many other members with many other designations who joined you in your last project. Basically, the point of enlisting all these positions is to highlight the challenge faced by a project manager. A project manager should at least have a mediocre understanding of all these realms.

Susanne was a project manager. She loved her job. She had quite a good understanding with her entire team. They adored her because she was not only an intelligent leader, but she was also an informed supervisor. She knew how to deal with different stakeholders. She also had quite a good understanding of efficient resource allocation and task distribution. However, she was a tad weaker at accounts. She understood basic accounts but got baffled when it came to big numbers and extensive budgeting.

Susanne very trustfully left that to her senior account manager and old acquaintance, Anthony. She relied heavily on his advice in all matters related to dollars. Since Susanne believed in rewarding her project team, Anthony religiously kept a side budget for bonuses and project closure parties. She thought he had to manage a very tight budget to make this allowance every time, and she thanked him sincerely for his cooperation.

Do you think Susanne is right to trust her account manager blindly? Are all Anthonys in your firm reliable and worthy of such a free reign?

Indeed, as a project leader, you do know of a few members who need strict surveillance. They might not necessarily betray your trust, but they may be known for occasionally flouting deadlines and not putting their complete efforts behind your cause.

Likewise, you don't know if Anthony ever shirked his responsibility or betrayed his team, but he did have all the chances. A tame lion left loose is still a lion: dangerous and unreliable. A team member without check and balance can any day become a Brutus.

Thus, a project manager must have a good command of all the processes. One does not expect the project manager to have absolute authority on every subject. At the end of the day, a specialized team member may know more of the issue than the project manager, and that is acceptable. As a project manager, you must have a "good" understanding of all the processes. You are the supervisor. You are also their mentor. How can you be a perfect guide and a good leader if you do not know all the processes you overlook?

Lastly, there are a few processes that are solely your domain.

- You are the issue resolver!
- You are the project initiator!
- You are also responsible for project closure!
- Your job does not end here.
- You are the team builder and motivator.

These are elements of your job description that are solely your department.

Domain III: Business Environment

Up till now, you have seen how project managers are bound to the people and processes and how they must learn to integrate both in their plans to gain success.

You have yet to discover the third domain. At first glance, you may feel the environment is external to the project. You may feel you had taken all the outsider influence into account when you appreciated the importance of all stakeholders.

However, the domain of the business environment is widespread.

Other than stakeholders, all your projects are burdened by the state's rules and regulations you operate in. Laws and statutes governing their actions bind all businesses. As a project manager, you must ensure your project is not overstepping the legal line. While digitizing your processes, you must ensure you are not giving way to mass unemployment or widespread unrest in your project team if they are reluctant to embrace change.

Secondly, you must chart out the widespread and long-lasting benefits of your project. Not only will it allow a proper appraisal of your project and its far-reaching benefits, but it will also help bring the stakeholders on board. Especially if, as a project manager, you are providing additional training to your project team, you must stress the benefit you are providing them by increasing their chances of employment in the future. If your project requires external funding, tracking down your project's benefits is a fool proof way to bring sponsors on board.

It is also likely that external and global occurrences impact your project. As a project manager, it is your responsibility to track such incidents and evaluate their impact on your business. Sometimes your project sponsor will also relay news of major external events to you. However, you must remember that you are responsible for upholding and maintaining the environment and the business hierarchies. All the news must travel through you.

Johnson was the project leader at his firm for four years, and he had the fortune to work with the same sponsor in all his consecutive projects. His sponsor would always take a keen interest in his project and its performance. Since Johnson updated all project developments on the cloud-based software, his sponsor was always in the loop. Every time there would be news of a change in the project plans, Johnson's sponsor would be the first to call him up. In fact, most times, the sponsor relayed his feedback before even the whole team saw the news. Over time, Johnson relied less on the regular news channels to keep his stakeholders informed and deemed the software updates sufficient. However, one time around, something disruptive happened.

Johnson placed his import order, and once the shipment hit the docks, he was informed of a new tariff imposed on imports from China. There was a change in trade regulations, and Johnson needed extra funds to release the stuck cargo. He updated the entire scenario on the software with a revised budget for the project and waited for the sponsor to approve it and give the green light. But, this time around, there was no response.

After two days, when Johnson called up the sponsor to get his approval on the revised budget, he was informed that the sponsor left the country the same morning for a family emergency and must have missed the budget changes due to an overworked schedule. Johnson was also informed that the approval could only be obtained once the sponsor returns since he does not want to be interrupted. The whole project got delayed for almost a week.

Who was responsible for the glitch? Obviously, Johnson. The sponsor was just doing a favor by following the project on the cloud, but the official channel for informing the sponsor should not have been abandoned. It is the job of the project manager to maintain the business hierarchy. Since he was accountable to the sponsor, he should have kept at least two to three official communication channels so that no news slips past without notice.

Lastly, project managers must remember that they and their team are part of a bigger organization. Though the project team is a whole unit with its independent operation, it is not distinct from the organization. The team will eventually be under the C.E.O. of the company and must follow the behavioral protocols set by the firm. The team must always keep the company's objectives at heart.

A successful project manager can instil this discipline in their team and align their team with its motto. They must make their team realize that the same way they are answerable to the project manager, the project manager, themselves, work under the larger banner of the company and cannot have conflicting interests with the organization.

The project team must have an appreciation for the entire chain of hierarchy. They must show loyalty and kinship for the whole organization and not just the project team.

Becoming a project manager is a challenging job, especially with all the technological advancements that are rapidly evolving the processes. It requires you to invest yourself in all three domains – people, processes, and environment – to climb the corporate ladder. A failed project manager can only bring about a failed project team and a failed project. The project manager is the sailor, and you must be the one to set the sails right to survive through bouncy waves and gusty winds.

PHASES

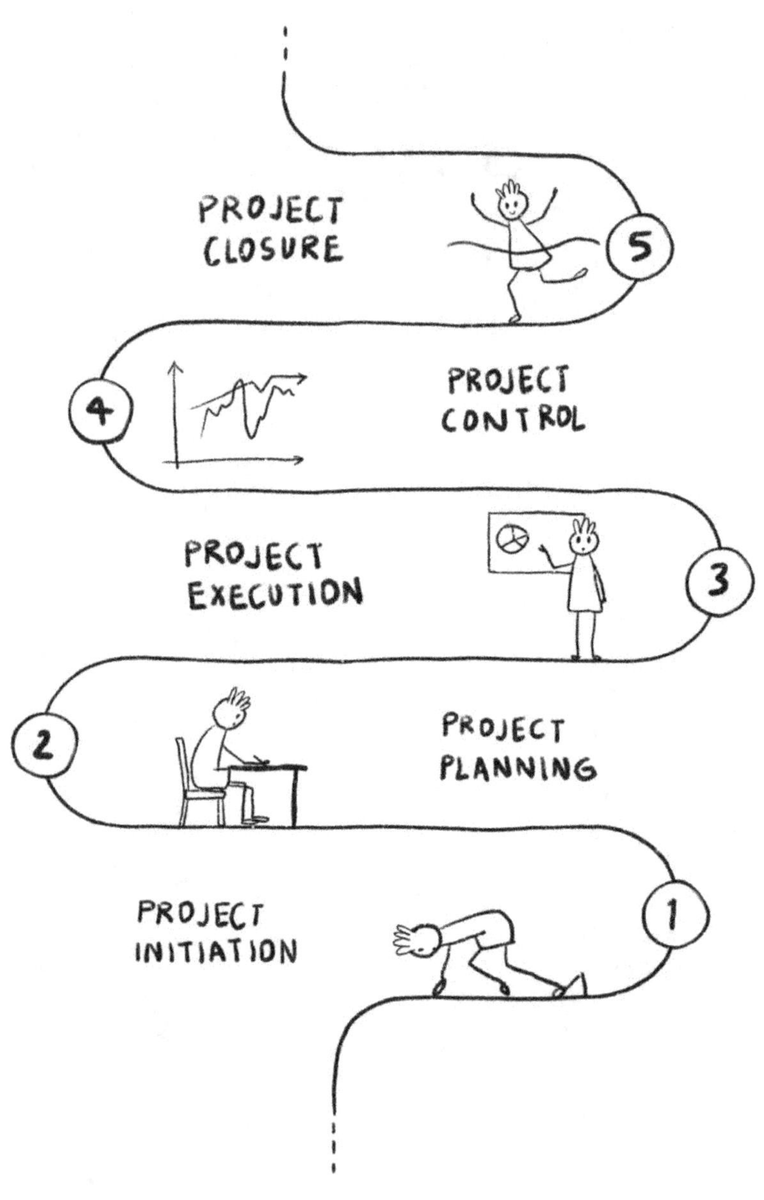

Enter Caption

Until now, you must have realized the importance of project management in achieving your target. It is the organized way of converging with a team to meet a set of common goals.

Every project has a set of milestones that can be defined as *phases of the project lifecycle.*

Confused? Let's first explore what a project lifecycle is!

A project lifecycle offers a bird's eye view of the project. It decides on the fundamentals of the project. Some questions that a project lifecycle should address include:

- What is the objective of the project?
- What sort of output should be expected at the project's end?
- What checkpoints should be observed at the end of each phase of the project?
- Who must participate in the project, and what domain would they work in?

Do you see how important each of these questions is to embark on a project? Just imagine a simple scenario where a family decides to renovate their kitchen. The father is the project manager, but he failed to outline the project lifecycle. Can you guess what will happen? The family would not know when the work was supposed to begin and when the carpenters would arrive. Thus, no one will make the kitchen space ready for when the workers arrive. The PM will also not be able to hold anyone accountable since he never assigned any responsibilities or designed a work schedule.

Likewise, no one will know when the plumbers will arrive and close off the water supply of the whole house before laying the pipes. It is likely that someone in the house will choose that moment to go for a bath and be disappointed with ceased water supply.

There will be a lot of fiasco but no one other than the PM will be to blame. Everyone will just shrug off accountability and reply, "we were never responsible for any job!" With this scenario, I guess you can see how difficult things would be if a PM fails to chart out a product lifeline? Everything will be haphazard. The team will feel constantly disoriented with no clear objectives to guide towards the desired end.

The greater chances are that the project will likely end unsuccessfully, and everyone will have bad memories to look back to.

5 Phases of Project Management

Since now you recognize the importance of sketching a project lifecycle, let's now talk about the phases of project management. A project lifecycle **outlines the project's primary objectives and will,** in most cases, chart out the team that will work on a given project. It presents the core objectives and deliverables of the project.

For example, a company suffered significant losses in the ongoing fiscal year. It decides to initiate a project to investigate the situation and to discover a course of action to correct it. Thus, the project lifecycle will firstly recognize a project manager and set out a general target. Likewise, it will decide what the objective of the project is. Is the objective only to discover the reason for the loss or devise a strategy to correct the loss? These are two different projects, and a project lifecycle must recognize what the project is striving for. Is it to achieve a tangible result in the form of an improved income statement or an intangible output in the form of a course of future action?

The first task of the PM is to recognize the object of the project. It may be perceived that the client will already have a clear idea of why they are engaging in project management. However, it is usually not so! The client depends on you to chart out the practicality of their objectives and to break it down into smaller manageable tasks.

Project management is basically the implementation of knowledge, skills, resources, and methodologies to various problems to reach a solution or fulfil the goals set forth. The phases of project management look closely into the steps and strategies that must be undertaken to meet the project's objectives. There are five phases for completing any project. These are stated below:

1. Project Initiation
2. Project Planning
3. Project Execution
4. Project Monitoring
5. Project Closure

For the moment, you may think this is an unnecessarily long way to go about completing a project and that you had been doing just fine until now. But don't you remember all the mini squabbles that came your way while you worked on a group project. Don't you ever remember being halfway through the project when you realized you had just run out of budget? Indeed, you are now nodding a yes.

Or it might have happened that when you thought you were done with the project, your client prompted you with reminders of so many small tasks left incomplete. It is also likely that halfway through the project, you realized you have misplaced all the documentation that charts your journey till now and either your bank is asking for it or the client needs it as proof of your expenditure. Now, you must be thinking it has happened more times than you would like. In fact, this is the same reason you start sweating when you hear of an upcoming project. Thus, it is vital to see a project through its different phases to obtain a smooth passage.

Let's look at all these phases in detail.

Phase 1: Project Initiation

Project Initiation, as the name suggests, will help you begin on a project. Not all projects are worth beginning!

You had an in-house meeting, and a new employee unwittingly suggested that you should diversify your business. Now instead of just producing leather products, you should run an entire farm. This way, you can have an in-house set of animals to give you a constant supply of hides. It is an idea, but not all ideas are worth a second thought. Do you think this was a valuable suggestion? You ask the other employees.

In the above case, as all the stakeholders replied with a definite no! For this purpose, the first phase of a project requires you to research the feasibility of a project.

Some people on the board thought the idea needed high investment, while others said that this would increase the cost of hides since the business will have to set up a whole new venture to source the hides. The maintenance cost of running a farm is also very high and will require a whole new set of skills. Some stakeholders said that the idea had a very high opportunity cost. The project was abandoned before it even began.

During the project feasibility testing, all the stakeholders of the project vote on the practicality of the project. After all, doing a project is not all theory. It consumes valuable resources. You will need to dedicate time, energy, and money. You will need to involve a whole bunch of people and arrange a working space for them to operate. These are just the very first few expenditures that must be undertaken to start a project.

For the project feasibility testing, you must first recognize all the stakeholders for a project. Then you must propose your project to them with all its objectives and goals. They may also require you to present estimates of cost and our work strategy. At this point, you do not have to be entirely accurate. However, the level of accuracy you grant will be indicative of your experience in the field.

Then you must gain the approval of all these stakeholders. If all of them agree on the project, the team will draw a Project Initiation Document (P.I.D.).

What should a P.I.D contain?

It will outline the critical components of a project. It should include the details of all the stakeholders and their degree of involvement in the project. A PID will also list the goal of the project and the reason for undertaking it. It will specify a budget and a timeframe for the project and recognize the project manager.

A PID will not include a lot of technicalities. It will just create the boundaries for initiating a project. The rest of the framework for executing the project will be crafted in the next phase: The Planning Phase.

Phase 2: Project Planning

The project planning Phase should be the most extensive because a project's success depends explicitly on it.

Unless you have a lot of experience being a project manager and have access to software like Agility, project planning can be a daunting task. It would require constant drafting and redrafting of project plans. Half of the project lifecycle is usually hogged by project planning. The more time and energy you spend in the planning phase, and the more soundly you predict risks, the higher is the probability that your project will go smoothly.

Before you start thinking about what goes into project planning, let's first look at the basis of making sound plans or goals. There are two ways to measure if your goals are practical and realizable.

You must first ensure that your goals are S.M.A.R.T. This measures if the goals are specific, measurable, attainable, relevant, and time-based. These five criteria are essential for making sound plans. The goals should be clearly defined. They should be achievable and measurable.

Let's look at goal setting in detail. Imagine that you work at a commission-based firm with a monthly basic pay of $300. You set a goal of increasing your monthly net income.

At this point, your goal is very vague. It does not specify how much you intend to increase your net pay, nor does it set the time frame in which you must achieve your goal, and neither does it outline a course of action to realize this aim.

In short, this goal is not S.M.A.R.T.

Now you must be wondering how you can make this goal of yours S.M.A.R.T. Let's start by looking at all these aspects in detail.

Specific: you would like to increase your monthly net pay by increasing the commission earned.

Measurable: you want to increase the monthly net pay to $600.

Attainable: this should test your goal in terms of its practicality. For example, your company has a basic pay cut-rate at $550. It has a clause that says commissions of up to $250 can be earned on the basic pay. That means your goal of making $600 is by no means attainable.

Relevant: Your goal and strategy must also be relevant. Assuming that you have a goal of increasing your net pay, you must also have a defined path to help you realize your goal. You aim to increase your commission earned by contacting more clients daily to make more sales. Or you may be struggling to improve your pitch to the customers so that you get more leads. This will make your goal relevant.

Time-Bound: Last but not least, your goal must be time-bound. A goal will have no importance if it is not in a time-restrain. You aim to increase your net pay but by when? Are you willing to wait a decade for it to happen? Or you want to see this increment within three months. It would help if you were very time specific.

These five criteria are very essential in charting out a goal that is realistic, practical, and worthy to be worked towards.

However, in the modern world, goals must be defined concerning different stakeholders and their interests. Thus, along with being S.M.A.R.T., the goals need to be C.L.E.A.R. too.

Collaborative: This allows the employees to work harmoniously together. Likewise, the P.M.s are required to be democratic while maintaining the Veto power.

Limited: This means that the goal should be clearly defined and then bound through the strands of budget and time. If the goals are not kept narrow, they can become unmanageable. Imagine if the goal is just to see an improvement in profits. The goal is not limited, and thus, the team may never know if they have realized the goal or not. There is no finish line in sight to encourage the employees to move forward.

An example of limiting the goal would be to see an improvement in profits within six months or to see a gain of $1000 in profits. Both these examples effectively restrict the goal.

Emotional: Emotional goals have become the need of modern times since employee satisfaction is a crucial pillar for success. The workers should be chosen based on their passion for the project. If the employees are disinterested in the task, they would not show innovation and drive to complete the project efficiently.

Appreciable: The bigger project should be dissected into small tasks to make them manageable. It also helps keep the workforce motivated.

Refinable: As you will see in the later phases of the project management lifecycle, there is much room for goals to swerve from the preset planning. Thus, the goals should be flexible.

During the planning phase, the scope of the project is set. The scope of the project refers to the final goals. During the goal setting, you would have seen that in specifying a goal, there are plenty of loose ends. For example, if the goal is closing up an operational factory, there can be multiple affairs resulting from this particular activity.

1. The existing workforce will find itself without employment.
2. The land of the factory will have to be sold or rented out. If the premises were rented for the factory, then the initial deposit may have to be recovered.
3. Likewise, accrued dues will have to be paid off.
4. Accounts of creditors and debtors will have to be settled.
5. The machinery will have to be sold off or rented out. Likewise, arrangements will have to be made for all the furnishings. If the factory is sold along with the furnishings and equipment, deeds of transfer will have to be drawn.

These were just a few examples of some loose ends resulting from the closure of a factory. The project planning phase must define what falls into the scope of the project. Is the project team only responsible for making arrangements for offloading the capital resources or the project management team will also be responsible for making alternate employment arrangements of the existing workforce? Is the project team also responsible for all the legal affairs arising out of this decision or this will be seen separately by the business's attorney?

It is essential to define what domains fall in the project manager's duties. This will directly impact the resources needed for the budget. Setting the scope of management is also essential in deciding the budget and the time needed for the project to bring it to completion.

Once the scope of the project is defined, it will act as a baseline for making other decisions about the project management. In fact, a project team can also be selected once the range of the project is set. Continuing the previous example, it is first important to decide whether the legal affairs will be dealt with by the project team or allotted separately to the business attorney. Only when this decision is made, can further decisions be made, like should the project team include an attorney or not!

Similarly, imagine that the project includes the responsibility of offloading the factory's equipment to the highest bidder. Thus, the project team should include someone with technical knowledge of the factory's machinery so they can correctly estimate their worth and help win a profitable bid.

Can you now see how important the project planning phase is for the success of the project?

The project planning stage will also include the setting up of timetables and specifying the deliverables. As you had studied in the definition of project management, project management refers to breaking up a complex project into small tasks and goals, to be achieved by the project team. The timetable will include the deadlines for the completion of small tasks that should together lead to the completion of the entire project.

The project planning stage will also specify the official channels of communication. Smooth and documented communication is a cardinal requirement for ensuring that the project progresses smoothly. A healthy communication network has many benefits.

It helps track essential information like who was responsible for which task, who proposed a specific idea, and who took responsibility for the now mishandled problem. This helps in managing a complex project team with many players. With the help of modern project management tools like an ERP cloud, tracing communication has become easier.

Additionally, specifying communication channels between stakeholders is also important. There should be immediate documentation of anything agreed to or discussed in meetings and sent out to all the concerned parties with the stamp of date and time. Similarly, all telephonic correspondences should be recorded and transcribed. If deemed important, copies of telephonic conversations should also be sent out. Can you imagine any more documentations that can smooth out the communication channels in extensive projects? Well, do you think that soft copies or hard copies alone are reliant forms of safekeeping data?

You must be thinking back to your fifth-grade lessons in the computer class when your teachers stressed on the importance of backups. For a big project with millions of dollars at disposal, and lots of stakeholders involved, it is the duty of the project management team to have plenty of backups of all their progress. This begins from the project planning phase.

Are you getting overwhelmed by all the technicalities of the planning phase? Do you think the list of requirements are enough to scare your team off?

It is your duty as a project manager to grill the importance of the planning phase in your team. The more circumspect your planning, the lesser likelihood of facing trouble during the project's lifecycle.

You may be wondering, what is the point of reiterating the upper statement again and again. The objective should be clear. It is to engrain the importance of this phase in your mind so that you can do the same for your team. Often, an under-experienced team is quick to leap into action. They want the thrill of the field and get easily bored of the theory. But beware! Having a weak theoretical base is the perfect ground to breed trouble. You will find yourself stuck over and over again in the execution phase. It is not uncommon to have revisions in the budget and timeframe of the project. However, if these revisions occur out of your inaccurate planning, it poses bad effects on your position as a project manager. If the real project is completely in conflict with your planning, your stakeholders may soon lose their trust in you. Their trust is essential in making the project sail smoothly.

Also, in the planning phase is the development of a *work breakdown structure (WBS)*. This overlooks the project in short episodes for effective team management.

Another important aspect of the Project Planning phase is the *change management plan*. As the name suggests, this involves the development of an effective strategy for managing sudden or unseen changes in the project plan. As repeatedly discussed, it is farfetched to assume that your project will never deviate from the planned trajectory since these projects exist in the highly volatile real world, they are susceptible to changes. Therefore, there must always be a plan to rain check major changes in the project. The change management plan charts out the course of action in cases of changes in the project. it signals out the responsible personnel for cartwheeling the changes. Obviously, it is the project manager who will sanction any changes in the project plan or the budget, but the change management plan presents the hierarchy for putting alternate plans in action. For example, if there is an alteration in the finances, who will correspond with the stakeholders, who will update the records, who will negotiate with the sponsors, who will hold the finances and be responsible to release payments. These honorary roles are all allotted during the planning phase to resist an anarchic situation in case of plan deviation.

Until now, you must be feeling hammered by so many obligations you must face in the planning phase but let's process all of them slowly. Look at the list below and see if you have all the documents ready for you to move on to the execution phase.

Scope Statement

A document that specifies the project's scope. It includes all technical details like the deliverables, the range of volatility, the budget, and the time frame for the project. It should also specify needs for different skills in the project team.

WBS: This schedule helps the team visualize the scope into small sections.

Milestones: Setting milestones help identify goals throughout the project to be met and you can also add them into your Gantt chart as tasks.

Gantt Chart: This will help you plan your task with timeline and person in charge for the work.

Communication Plan: This helps in messaging stakeholders in and out of the project and you can also make timelines of what and when depending on your tasks and deliverables.

Risk Management Plan: This will help you recognize potential risk. You might include risk of variation in cost and delivery time or budgets. You may also find customer reviewing and feedback processes as something that can cause delay and risk to project delivery. Other risks can be the shortage of resources.

As the PM, it was a big day for Addison. He was about to present the upcoming project to his team. Americana Towers was proposed to become a residency whose security system was to be digitized with an automatic alarm system to become the safest zone on Earth.

Clarkson was one of the major stakeholders who was funding the project and Addison was expecting a project cost of $10 million per floor. Addison presumed that his impeccable project planning will effectively diffuse all the constraints and hopefully the panel will agree with his overall project strategy.

"Well, I say you must keep in mind that this is New York Mr. Addison. And if this is the spot you've chosen then you must know that here you might have to spend $15 million per floor." Charlie exclaimed. He was one of the major sponsors of the project.

"Yes, I agree with Mr. Charlie. Nevertheless, you can have security running on a 100-story structure in Chicago at the same cost. Are you sure you are choosing the right location, Mr. Addison?" Clarkson interrupted the conversation.

"I must say you all are prepared with questions and concerns, which is good." Addison smiled as he spoke. "However, I can assure you that New York is the best place for the launch of this project. We can decrease the number of floors for the tower for now and will keep adding to them as the project finds favor with the investors."

All the stakeholders gave in to the self-assurance exuded by Addison.

However, as the project reached its execution phase, Addison's budget saw three revisions. Addison had under-evaluated the travelling cost of the engineers. He had also failed to include the import duties on the specialized machinery he got imported from Germany. As a result, Addison had to face constant reprimands from the sponsors. His estimations were so out of league that Addison could only put up seven floors out of ten and even then, the security system was not as grand as advertised. The project lost its USP and failed on major commitments.

This project taught a major lesson to Addison. He realized he should have invested more time and energy in the project planning and also kept a buffer for unseen scenarios when estimating the project's budget.

Do you see the repercussions of being hasty and negligent during the project planning phase? Don't expect the sponsors and the stakeholders to approve of every swerve in the plan just because they are committed to the project. When you were warned of revisions in the project plan and budget, you were not discussing merrily about an increment of a few dollars. These projects are major undertakings and any revision in cost usually refers to a divergence of about million dollars from the original proposition. Thus, no matter how committed the stakeholders are to the project they would not easily give in to every change in the project's plans. Therefore, you must be vigilant when drawing up the project plan.

Phase 3: Project Execution

What follows the planning phase is the Project Execution phase. This is where things actually happen. Until now, you were engrossed in defining and designing the project, but now it's time to bring it all into perspective. Here you will receive semi-finished and finished deliverables.

This phase too begins with a meeting. The goal of the conference is to "Kick-start" the work. All the planning that went into the earlier stage is put to fruition as the primary project team is split into small groups, each with its own dedicated tasks and goals.

Since now everybody is busily working on different tasks, a reporting channel becomes critical. There should be a proper system of submitting status reports, attending performance meetings, and providing updates on project development to ensure that the entire team is working congenitally towards a common end.

A list of tasks necessary during the project execution phase includes

1. Systematically organizing team
2. Distributing and managing resources
3. The Project Manager should overlook the team
4. Keep tabs on the project's entire crew
5. Dividing tasks to ensure efficient time and energy management
6. Organize weekly or biweekly meetings. These could be more or less frequent as the need arises.
7. Make any alterations in project deadlines or project plans.

Though the schedule of the project and project plans are already crafted in the project planning stage, sometimes halfway during the project execution, PM may realize a need for the alternation in the plans. However, he should keep a complete and thorough check on his team to ensure that no delays or problems arise from the team's inefficiency.

Along with organizing meetings to check on the team's performance, a modern-day solution would include having a shared cloud-based software to share updates on the projects in real-time. This would allow the team members to feel connected to the entire PM team and create a drive to compete and complete goals within the assigned deadline.

This solution would also reduce the need for full-house meetings with the team since they can get really long as each group updates on their individual progress. As the team already has a shared forum to connect, the PM can now organize small meetings with different specialized groups as needed rather than calling everyone together and wasting precious time.

Phase 4: Project Performance/Monitoring

In phase 3, you saw that despite intensive planning, the project plans may get disrupted. But the question is, what do you mean by changes in project plans, and how will these changes affect the project's success?

There are five key indicators for measuring the success of the project. A PM will use any two of the four Key Performance Indicators (KPI) to measure the project's success. Which KPIs would the PM use should be decided from the beginning, preferably during the planning phase. This reduces the chance of biasedness, which may arise if the choice of KPI is made later, as the PM may feel inclined to choose a measure that reflects higher success.

1. **Project Objectives:** this indicator measures if the project is on time and has abided by the budget designated by the stakeholders.
2. **Effort and cost tracking:** this KPI measures the efforts made by the team to complete the task on time and within the budget. It sees if the efforts align with the other targets because if the efforts fall short, the costs may arise during the project's life. However, it is critical that employees' performance was not overestimated during the planning phase. For example, you have a project to produce 500 leather jackets, and your team can make 50 jackets per day. Then, assuming that your team can accomplish that goal in 7 or 8 days is an unfair estimation of the project's lifespan. This disregards the S.T.E.M. and CLEAR goals.
3. **Milestones:** this measures the percentage of deadlines missed during the life of the project. Since the project is divided into small tasks, if all these tasks are completed in time, the project will likely be done in time.
4. **Project performance:** this KPI measures the frequency of unexpected hurdles coming along the way. These indicate two things. It would indicate the efficiency of planning during the planning phase. If the planning were precise, the number of unforeseen circumstances would reduce significantly. Secondly, it measures the skill and resourcefulness of the team in averting crisis. If the unit is experienced, it will handle all the problems with haste while sticking to the given time constraint and budget.

Phase 5: Project Closure

This phase is the most rewarding one. Team members outsourced from outside are released from the contract. The in-house team members are honored for their valuable contribution and appraised for their performance.

At times, a project completion party may also be celebrated to relax the team members after a strenuous project. However, project closure is not always festivities and merriment.

Mainly after each project's end, there will be a project appraisal meeting. In this meeting, the team evaluates its strengths and weaknesses during the journey. This 'post-mortem' meeting also involves brainstorming ways to improve the team's performance in the future.

Lastly, the PM, along with their crew, will make final reports on the project. These reports will showcase the actual expenditure on the project, the diversion from the original budget, and a final evaluation of the project's deliverables.

The project is effectively closed only once all the stakeholders approve of all the deliverables. All of them must give their stamp of approval. Your Gantt chart should also display 100% completion of all the phases. The backups of the project's processes and activities must also be effectively created and distributed to the concerned parties.

If any of the project's tasks were left incomplete during the project's lifecycle, they too would be completed now in the closure phase.

CHAPTER SIX

PROBLEMS

Enter Caption

In the previous chapters, you have read about how 'project management is an approach that guides you towards leading a project efficiently. Thus far, this book has set an emphasis on two things.

a. As a project manager, you must develop skills at a personal level to ensure that your leadership of a project is on the right track.
b. And how you can employ various software, tools, strategies, and methods to ensure that your project implementation goes smoothly.

Project Management as a complete business case

Apart from these two key takeaways, you must understand that project management is a discipline that plays a crucial role in business management. Entrepreneurs and organizations often overlook the crucial role of project management. The traditional business development and management idea emphasizes the foundational roles of human resources, finance, or general operations. Setting up a project management department is not often the first thing a small startup or company will do.

That is a big mistake.

A designated project management department or a project manager plays a central role in decision-making and task execution.

A common misconception amongst people is that 'project management is just a skill that managers and leaders must employ. You might be one of those people. If you are, then you need to take a step back.

While it is true that project management is indeed a skill that you need to inculcate to become an effective leader, there is more to it.

Project management is a particular discipline that requires rigorous training and experience. A successful project management department collaborates with other departments to create realistic goals consistent with an organization's culture, needs, and strategies. In short, it makes sure that any new initiative or idea is implemented in a structured and cohesive manner.

Many people believe themselves to be skilled at project management because they are insightful and intuitive leaders, but the full scope of project management goes beyond this. Project management is not different from any other professional discipline.

Think about it. In your lived experience, what does project management mean to you?

More often than not, you will notice that businesses try to take shortcuts with project management by treating it lightly and casually. Consultants trained in project management encounter clients who believe in old-fashioned ideas of 'specialization' and 'division of labor. They expect each executive manager or leader to excel at their jobs individually. They expect some level of coordination but nothing much beyond that. Undermining the role of a proactive project management department that guides the future course with the correct procedures, insight, and structure is a mistake you don't want to make.

Even at an individual level, if you are a single person leading a personal project, you need to focus on project management just as closely as you would on budgeting, marketing, etc.

Let's look at an example of a fintech startup, XPay.

A group of young entrepreneurs has come together with the idea of developing an app that offers special discounts to students from a selection of vendors. The team of four co-founders is computer science students who are experts at coding and programming.

They have successfully created a mobile application with a user-friendly interface after multiple trials and errors. The only thing remaining is to start marketing their product by highlighting its utility to i) students and ii) vendors.

They divide the tasks amongst each other; Sam and Thomas take responsibility for technical upgrades to the application, Wendy takes responsibility for marketing, and Mary becomes the CEO of the small startup. They run their idea through a business incubation program that connects them with veteran business leaders and benefits from their mentorship. It seems that XPay is off to a great start.

XPay decided to launch itself into the market by applying to a government-funded program that sponsors young startups. The requirements of the program are rigorous and require a lot of effort on everyone's ends. Here we start to notice some hiccups. The passionate young group of people does good jobs on their ends, but their efforts seem not to yield the best outputs.

Each of them encounters an individual level of issues and problems, which puts them in challenging positions. After all, they are a group of programmers and not project management specialists or business studies majors.

Let's look at one of their problems.

Wendy is reaching out to different universities, schools, and students to conduct a small survey that provides factual data showing that XPay is a business solution that the market needs. She quickly makes an online survey with a basic set of questions and sends it out. With a small deadline window, she has to move quickly. She reaches out to several student clubs and administrative representatives at three different universities.

However, she grows increasingly concerned due to the lack of response to the survey. With not enough data, she has no backup plan. How do they show that they have conducted preliminary market research?

In the meantime, Sam and Thomas don't have a lot of responsibility apart from introducing minor upgrades in the application to make it more user-friendly and easier to use. When the entrepreneurs decide to meet to discuss their progress, Wendy informs every one of her lack of progress.

How differently would this go if there was a project manager on board? What would you do differently? Start noting down the suggestions that immediately pop up in your mind and revisit them later.

Here is the first thing a project manager could lend support with: identify goals. Wendy sent out the survey quickly, but there is a meticulous process to design a good survey. The set of questions she designed quickly were not precise and well-worded. A leader who is not from a marketing background cannot be expected to know what a business expert is looking for when evaluating XPay's application.

Designing a survey should have been outsourced to a business expert and reviewed by any of the mentors that XPay's team met during the incubation program.

Second, a project manager would establish a proper reporting channel where every one of the team members shared their progress. You might be wondering why the group was not doing this.

It is not a matter of simple coordination. First, a project manager would design SMART goals for everyone. Second, they would ensure that everyone prioritizes the right tasks and shares any hiccups right from the start. Gathering preliminary research is a goal that the entire team needs to achieve. If Wendy runs into problems with that, it will impact XPay's ability to get the sponsorship, not just hers. With that in mind, a project manager would ensure the completion of the proper milestones on time.

Reallocating tasks to Sam and Thomas, who were not dealing with any urgent technical upgrades, would have been an excellent course of action. By combining the team's time and efforts, more data could be gathered from a larger sample of people.

Lastly, a project manager would have guided Wendy through a problem-solving exercise once it became apparent that lack of response was an issue. By brainstorming the possible reasons why people did not respond to the survey, Wendy could introduce countermeasures to ensure that more people willingly filled out the survey.

A well-articulated survey that takes very little time to finish often does better than a lengthy survey (in terms of the number of questions and/or the detailed scenario-based questions). In addition to that, Wendy had to ensure that everyone who was asked to fill the survey *knew* that it would be done quickly. A project manager could have supported Wendy by efficiently addressing every problem she encountered with several other solutions.

Does Wendy's ability to address the unexpected problem reflect her poor project management skills? Not at all.

This example highlights the need to take a project manager on board to facilitate goal setting and target achievement. An entrepreneur will have the proper guidance and support from a properly trained expert specializing in project management. Even though XPay was an initiative by a group of creative individuals who did not lack determination or passion, they required feedback from a project manager who could support them in becoming successful.

Take a moment to think about your solutions before this section elaborates on what a project manager would have done. Did you learn something new? Do you have more innovative solutions to offer? What do you think you would do differently?

Conduct Assessment: A Continuous Process

Project Management is a versatile discipline that focuses on various areas; one of them is problem-solving. Unexpected scenarios keep popping up everywhere, especially for leaders who manage and coordinate with different-sized teams. A coordinator supervising a team of two people will face problems just as much as a Regional Manager of Unilever with multiple teams of hundreds of people reporting to him.

Project Management does not discriminate between the problems that you face. The first thing a project manager will start with once they encounter a problem of any level is: examine and assess.

The first questions to inquire about off the bat are:

- What's the problem?
- Who is it affecting?
- What's causing the problem?
- What are the effects and impacts of the problem?

- Are there any unexpected outcomes of this problem?
- Who can resolve the problem?
- Would the proposed solutions have any unexpected outcomes?

It is essential to ask questions that allow you to understand problems comprehensively and in full detail. Importance of perceiving problems is fundamental to problem-solving. You cannot design an intervention or introduce a creative solution if you don't fully understand the situation.

Take a deep divide into the situation. Just imagine that you are inside a 3D simulation where everything around you is frozen in place. You are walking through the scenario, poking and prodding in different places to increase your knowledge about the situation.

Let's elaborate further on conducting assessment through various visualization exercises in the next section. Keep reading further to learn how to creatively understand your problems, not much different than imagining yourself inside a 3D simulation.

Problem-Solving Through Visualization – Fish Diagram

As a project manager, you will come across various situations where you will struggle to identify problems and the factors causing those problems. In such a moment, you can utilize the fishbone exercise to alienate the factors contributing to a problem from the problem itself.

The fishbone exercise, more commonly known as the Ishikawa Diagram, is easy to visualize and analyze the cause-and-effect relationship between various factors.

Let's try to learn this exercise through an example. Consider the case of Anna, working as a PM for a clinical trial at a hospital.

Anna has been working as a Program Manager at a Public Healthcare and Research facility for a year. On a busy Monday morning, she is called into the office by her Head of Department, Steve. She is ushered into the clean and spacious office of Steve and handed a tightly bundled up file. Steve looks up, hands clasped together, and says, "There is a new project, and I want you to take a look at it. It's a short-term project, and I think you are ready to handle this. Review and let me know what you think."

Anna thanks him and walks out of the office. She grabs a quick cup of coffee and starts looking through the file. The project is a new clinical trial for herbal medicine, an effective cure for the common cold and flu. The institute that Anna works at has to research the efficacy of herbal medicine by testing it on people and analyzing the results.

As the Monday morning shifts into the afternoon, Anna quickly reviews the file, sipping her coffee and highlighting essential sections to revisit later. The brief once-over she gives to the file is enough to mentally divide the project into three stages: planning, execution, and reporting.

It seems easy enough to her. In the past, Anna has tirelessly worked on several projects and gained valuable experience in managing operations, logistics, and administrative tasks.

Anna reaches into her drawers, pulling out a loose sheet of paper. She scribbles a couple of details for future reference, figuring out that the project duration will be three months, and she will need to recruit 300 participants to conduct the study. Feeling a surge of motivation, she makes a decision.

By later afternoon, she knocks on Steve's door and goes inside when he ushers her in through the glass window. One step into the office, and she informs, "I have taken a look at the project file, and I will do it. Just let me know when we should have a detailed meeting about this so we can get started."

Steve nods, "I will let you know when we can have a meeting. Expect it to be tomorrow morning."

The next day, Anna has everything outlined and ready to be put into the process. She makes detailed plans to understand the process and the timeline. For the next two weeks, she pulls all-nighters to develop a comprehensive, step-by-step plan to ensure that she can execute the project efficiently.

Once she has arranged all the logistical and human resources, she realizes a major problem she did not consider. To carry out the investigation, she has to find willing participants who will partake in the study and provide timely feedback to test the medicine's effectiveness.

However, a basic marketing campaign including flyers and advertisements is not enough. Anna had earlier thought it would be an appropriate marketing strategy, but something seems to be not working.

Here is her problem then. How can she solve it?

After spending a whole afternoon worrying about this problem, she comes to a dead end. There are just too many factors contributing to the problem, and she is overwhelmed by the multiple explanations her mind is conjuring up. She sighs deeply, looking resigned and ready to ask Steve to step in and help her out.

She hears a noise behind and a loud chuckle. Spinning around on her chair, she sees the face of her colleague Samantha who takes one look at Anna and raises a curious brow. After listening to everything, Samantha just nods her head in understanding and offers advice.

"Try to visualize the problem. The thing is, you have too many ideas floating about your head, and writing it all down might not help because it's a big dump of words. Why don't you do the fishbone exercise?"

Slightly intrigued, Anna remarks, "Oh yeah, I remember doing that in college for a research project. That's probably a good idea, Sam! Let me try it and see where everything goes."

Considering that most of the target audience of clinical trials tends to come from working-class backgrounds and daily wage workers, Anna grabs a chart paper and draws the basic diagram. For understanding, take a look at the reference image below.

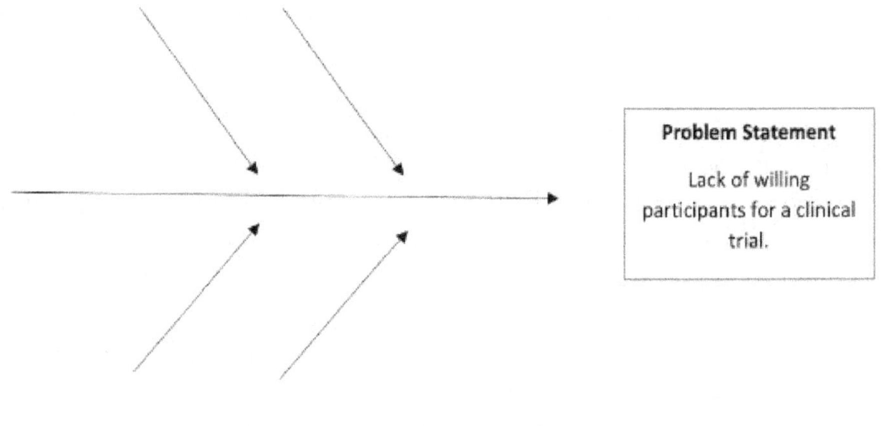

Enter Caption

On the four corresponding arrows, Anna begins to write down what she believes is the cause of this problem. She outlines the following reasons:

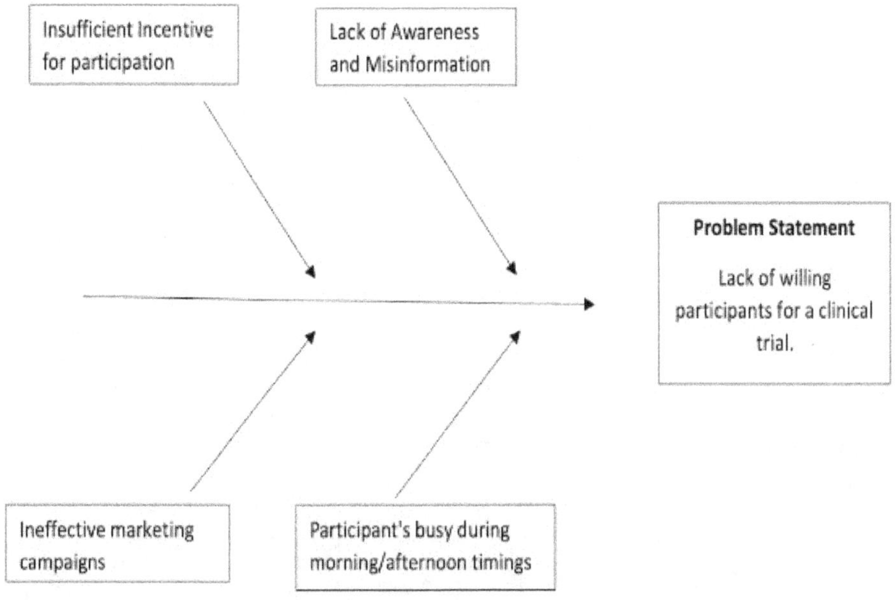

Enter Caption

Once she has outlined the leading causes, she starts to branch out further to understand what's causing these issues. Once she is done, her fish diagram looks something like this.

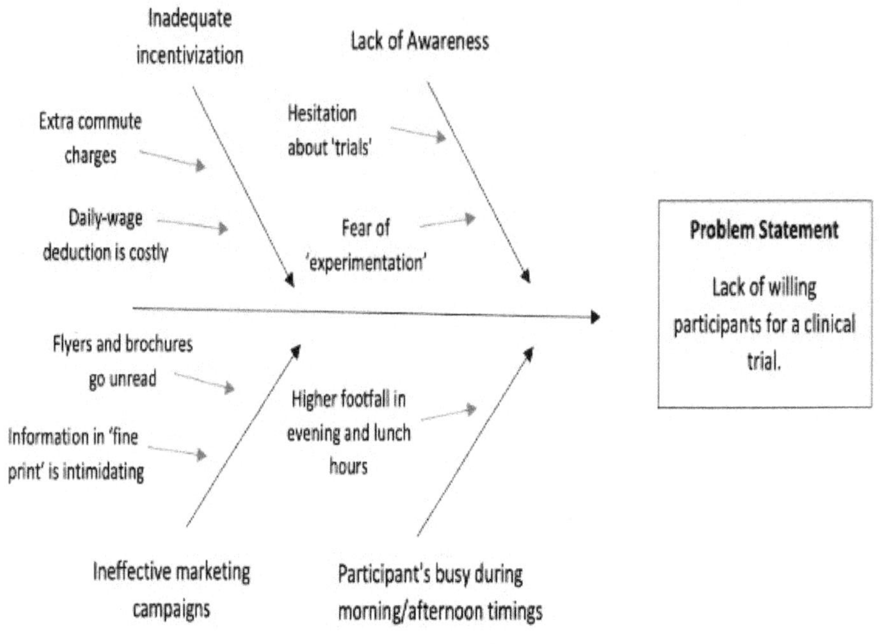

Enter Caption

Anna keeps adding details and pointers to the diagram.

Once she has fleshed out every single problem, she looks at the chart with a proud glint in her eyes. She feels that she understands her project better now. Looking at the detailed map, she feels a surge of certainty that she can enroll more participants in her study with a few interventions. She gets her friend Sam to review the fish diagram, who points out a couple of points that Anna did not consider. Grateful for Sam's support, Anna packs up and leaves for home.

The next day, she starts coming /up with different solutions to counter the problems she has outlined. Are you curious to find out how she designed the countermeasures? What are the ideas that you have in mind?

Designing Countermeasures & Risk Management

Once you have understood the ins and outs of the problem you are encountering, the problem assessment is over. Now you can focus on problem-solving.

Designing effective countermeasures is a rigorous and challenging process. You have to come up with intelligent solutions that are easily implementable. Although you can quickly come up with long and drawn-out solutions, what you need is a plan that offers the shortest and most efficient route. Try to find a solution that directly addresses the root cause of problems leading to project failure. Don't mistake this with taking a shortcut – interventions that are not thorough and well-defined often fail.

Once you have a couple of interventions in mind, you will need to flesh them out by outlining the tools, methods, and processes used to execute them successfully. As a project manager, you will soon realize that the more robust your level of planning will be, the better off you will be.

Figure out the requirements, calculate your next moves, and set goals to achieve your targets once again. Work on building a framework or rubric that will test the effectiveness of the interventions once they are underway. You have to closely monitor and evaluate your progress to ensure that you are going in the right direction.

It's crucial to possess the ability to foresee future challenges that can hinder your project's overall progress. If you fail to adopt solutions without planning out other risk prevention measures, you might be caught unprepared by sudden challenges. Even if you have a very detailed plan, it is pretty likely that it will not go according to it. Usually, project managers have to keep a margin of flexibility and adjustability in project implementation. That's why it is vital to keep a risk management plan that supports you with strategies to mitigate unexpected hindrances.

Often, to build a solid plan, you need to utilize the expertise of experienced leaders who specialize in your field, or you need to enlist a skilled project manager. If you cannot do that, then make sure you leave no stone unturned. Keep learning new ways to improve your project management skills. With dedicated effort, you will be able to lead a project to successful completion.

When you are planning different interventions, keep the following points in mind:

- Is your proposed solution SMART? (Specific, measurable, achievable, realistic, and time-bound)
- Who will the intervention impact?
- Could the intervention cause any unexpected outcomes or problems?
- Are there any reasons that it can fail? If so, what are they?

- Have other people before you used similar solutions? If yes, how did it work out for them?

It cannot be stressed enough, but: do your research. You will save yourself time, energy, and resources if you approach the problem with sure-footed countermeasures.

Case Study: Brainstorming Solutions

Let's continue the case of Anna and her clinical trial to see how she devised solutions to counter the problems she faced.

The following day, she kept researching different ways to resolve the four leading causes she outlined earlier. Her Google search history is full of various reports about other clinical trials involving herbal medicine. She primarily focuses on the reports' sampling and data collections sections to understand how others tackled the same issues. She discovers that clinical trials often support community healthcare workers who go door-to-door in their neighborhoods to recruit participants. It has proven to be an effective and low-cost investment. With this intervention, she will target two main problems she highlighted earlier, i.e., spread awareness and reduce misinformation.

Satisfied with this idea, she starts brainstorming on ways to tackle the following two problems.

After a small lunch break, she starts reading different articles and blogs on incentivizing participants without requesting a large chunk of extra funding. Trying to incentivize the participants by suggesting that they contribute to a more significant cause is not enough. The marketing campaign on the flyers and brochures tried to use 'the greater good' as a selling point, but it did not work.

Anna's mind runs in circles, trying to circumvent this problem. She can request monetary incentives from the sponsors, but she has to ensure that the amount is limited because then there will be a higher chance of revised budget approval.

She decides to experiment with offering minimal transport costs to the participants. Unsure whether or not it will work, she asks one of her research associates to call ten participants to gauge their response. Surprisingly, it works out, and six out of ten people agree readily to participate in the trial. However, four people express concerns about the timing, wanting to come during the evening instead of the morning or afternoon. Looking at this feedback, Anna quickly decides to change the timing of the trial from afternoon to late evening. It seems that this was the most straightforward solution she could think of.

Once she has her ideas ready, she types out a quick report and runs it by Steve, her supervisor.

He nods approvingly at her proposal, "You have done a thorough job, I believe. Make a revised budget, and let's try to get it approved by the sponsors. If they refuse, you can go ahead with changing the time and utilize field officers to strengthen community engagement."

Anna smiles and nods back in affirmation. She goes back to her desk and gets started on drafting another proposal that the sponsors will review. She begins by outlining the problem statement and then outlines the proposed interventions in detail. Her plan is thorough and takes into account different risks that might render her interventions ineffective.

The suggestion to introduce monetary incentives is costly for the sponsors and might be rejected. Knowing that Anna decides to base her incentivization plan for participants on other factors. She offers to take onboard the doctors and consultants who agree to provide free consultations to participants if they experience any side effects relating to the herbal medicine while they are part of the trial. Knowing that there will hardly be any side effects, it is free of cost intervention that plays a crucial role in making participants feel comfortable and secure.

Furthermore, to reduce the number of monetary incentives, Anna asks the field officers to target communities in areas closer to the research site.

In three days, she has everything ready and a presentation set up for the sponsors. What do you think happens? It does not come as a surprise when Anna gets the approval.

Based on the thorough research and planning, the sponsors decided to accept the slight increase requested in the offered budget. Ecstatic, Anna is relieved and grateful for the hard work she put into resolving the problem that arose. The fish diagram was the first step she took towards problem assessment, and the rest was history.

STORIES

Enter Caption

During the past few chapters, you went through the various technicalities of project management. Until now, you must have collected a thorough idea of what your role as a project manager entails. You must have also recognized the pitfalls you must avoid.

Throughout, there remained a stress on how to become a "good project manager." Being a project manager is never enough. Being a PM is not a solo ride. Though it may be included in the list of general professions, it is highly performance-based. If you are a teacher, you may demonstrate low levels of energy a particular week and still suffer no consequences. If you are an accountant, you may exhibit laziness in updating books for a few days, yet, be able to deliver updated and accurate year end accounts. You may buckle up your performance before you are asked to present the financial reports. If you are a writer, you can be excused for having writer's blocks. In most jobs, you can also call for a sick leave or holiday leave, without suffering any repercussions.

However, a few professions require higher levels of self-control. One cannot excuse a lackluster performance and hope to extend their contract. Can you imagine a few such occupations?

What about a surgeon?

Or a fighter pilot?

Even a professional chess player is bound to lose the game if his attention dwindles for a few minutes.

Likewise, the success of a project is highly reliant on the project manager. Do you know what that means? If a project manager enters the office and pays no attention to his whereabouts and his team, there are high chances that soon the project will derail.

Let's look at some stories that best illustrate the point I'm trying to make.

Brian

The project planning phase usually undertakes the strength and efficiency of each team member before determining deadlines. That means it depends on everyone's complete dedication and contribution to the project. Thus, if the project manager shows a lapse in judgement and attention, it is likely that either the team will also demonstrate inefficiency, or the team may feel lost without attention. Both can translate only into three outcomes:

- Flouting of the time frame,

- A disregard of the pre-set budget
- Or in the least, a deterioration in the quality of the deliverables.

Obviously, all three outcomes indicate only one thing: the project has failed.

However, take heart! It is normal for projects to require repetitive revisions of budget and deadlines. Especially, if the risks are not well-assessed during the planning phase, there is a strong probability that the plans will have to be modified as the project progresses through the execution phase. Hence, as a project manager, it is your duty to ensure that the modifications in the budget and deadlines are occurring not because of inefficiency on part of the project team, but due to the unpredictability faced during the project.

The project planning phase must be completed with absolute attention to all project hurdles and with the last deliverables in sight. The tangible or intangible outcome of the project should also be clearly envisioned for smart planning. Do you remember the S.M.A.R.T and C.L.E.A.R goals you studied about in the planning phase? As a PM, be very attentive that the goals your team has collectively set fulfill all the criteria of effective goals. Failing to do so can have a negative impact on the performance of your team. In the example below, Brian failed to lead his team with precision, and he suffered for his mismanagement.

The hot and humid Monday morning had started slowly. As Brian worked through his morning routine, he realized that this week would be hectic and tiring, but he had to power through all the meetings and discussions.

The last weeks had been exhausting because Brian had somehow stayed back in his office every day. Sipping half-finished and cooling cups of coffee, Brian reviewed multiple performance reports of his team to analyze ways to achieve an increased productivity level. To say he was slightly frustrated would be untrue - he was scratching the bottom of the barrel. Last week, he had designated a deadline-sensitive task to his team. Designing software is a demanding process, but for Brian, it was a question of meeting deadlines.

Brian finished drinking his morning coffee and grabbed his car keys to leave for the office with all these thoughts swimming through his head. Once he got out of the dining elevator, he looked at all his team members, expecting everyone to be at the office right on time. Unfortunately, even that day three employees were late. He frowned as he saw the ones who had arrived, lounging about on their desks. He muttered a "good morning" and heard some half-hearted greetings back in response before he went inside his office. Setting his stuff down, his forehead was marred by a deep-set frown. Picking up the phone, he dialed the extension for Rohan, a senior software engineer.

He started with a stern tone, "We are having a meeting in half an hour to take a progress update on our current project."

Rohan replied rather inaudibly," Yes sir, of course. I will let everyone know."

For half an hour, Brian checked the progress himself and deduced the quality of work to be extremely disappointing. By the time the meeting rolled around, Brian had reached a peak of frustration.

Once everyone settled down, he started by addressing the elephant in the room.

"We need to talk about the snail's pace we have been taking with this project. I don't understand what's the delay. You people don't seem to understand even the basics."

Brian looked around at each face, expecting a response but when everyone held on steadfastly to silence, he couldn't help but growl in frustration.

"Well, will anybody bother to answer? Can you all individually report the recent progress you made?"

Kane Riley, Jennifer Sean and Mike Steve piped together,

"I tracked down the different stakeholders as we discussed in the last meeting."

"I got the list of stakeholders ready."

"I got into contact with our biggest stakeholder."

As it turned out, three project members had dedicated their precious time in completing a single task. There was a misuse of human resources.

"You all did the same work? Why did no one assign duties among yourselves?"

As it turned out, no matter how stringent Brian was about organizing biweekly meetings, he did not design specific goals and delegate individual tasks. He just charted out the general weekly goals and expected everyone to choose their share of the workload.

He was hoping for a utopian world, where pieces will automatically fall into place. However, he had failed to underline the particulars of the project. He may have successfully broken down the greater goal into small achievable and measurable tasks, but he had not assigned duties or placed anyone in charge to complete the tasks within the time allotted. Thus, everyone waited for the other to take the lead and in doing so nobody made any progress.

After looking at failure in face, he decided to get the help of a project management software. Instead of collecting the entire project team in the conference team every week and spending hours debriefing everyone about the project's pace and the upcoming targets, he started maintaining records on the ERP.

The time he earlier dedicated to heading meetings was better allocated in delegating individual tasks to the project team through the cloud. The specialized software sent customized mails to every employee, designating their daily and weekly tasks.

The members too were required to log on their progress on the ERP. As the project propelled forward, the software's home page displayed statistical data of the project completion for everybody's benefit. The statistics were presented as a Gantt chart that you saw in chapter 5 and will study in further detail in the addendum.

Now, Brian met individually with each team member to assess their performance and solve their queries. After the installation of an ERP, most employees thanked Brian. They said they were feeling useless on the team earlier, since they never knew what to do and who to report to. Every day they used to spend about an hour wastefully, scrambling for which task to pick. They had started feeling like an excess to the project team. They also felt that Brian was intentionally withholding work from them, thinking only himself to be competent enough to deal with the client.

They said that though after the introduction of ERP, the frequency of inhouse meetings had largely reduced, they felt better connected to the team and the project by observing the live updates on the Gantt Chart.

Brian too felt that the Gantt Chart had made it easier for him to keep tabs on the team's performance. He could also now prioritize tasks to be performed while postponing the non-essential task for during project closure. This helped him meet the project deadlines in time.

Here was one example how adaptation and application of a project management software helped avert a crisis.

US Airways and American Airlines

Another real-life example is that of the merger of US airways and American Airlines. This horizontal merger resulted in duplication of technology and resources since both the companies operated in the same field and had their own fully-fledged operations. Once they merged under a single banner, they had to efficiently free up overlapping resources to make the operations more effective.

The directors knew that the task could not be accomplished through simple data entry in spreadsheets. Thus, a project team came into existence which looked closely into capitalizing 20% of the labor instead of 10% which may have appeared the obvious choice at first sight. However, a close insight into resource management delivered a different solution. The newly emerged company managed to maintain its operational capacity while reducing its expenses by many million dollars. The proposed project managed to increase the company's efficiency by multifold things that could not have been done without successful project management.

Charlie Thompson

Projects are complex undertakings. Not only do they deal with critical affairs that the organization cannot tackle on its own, but these projects also rely on a temporary project team that emerges just to fulfill the project. A temporary project team brings challenges of its own. Everyone on the team must recognize the new authority and work with dedication for the project. Everyone must also believe in the necessity of the project to be undertaken. A project team may also possess a hierarchy of its own where positions are reversed from the actual positions in the organization. All the team members must adopt and accept the new roles. Sometimes, external candidates, ones who are not part of the organization, may also need to join the project team. They are usually expert consultants brought in for their experience and expertise regarding the new project. Hence, the project team must welcome the outsourced talent with warmth and appreciate their role. For a project to be successful, there need be no power politics.

Charlie Thompson started working as a project manager in July and approached his first days on a scale factor. So, the first 2-3 days he took to familiarize himself with the company, the processes, the culture and control documents floated while managing a project. He then took 2-3 days to do the same with the customer and other stakeholders and about 9 days in total to get fully onboard with his projects. He realized the importance of a compact and unified project team. He thought a well-bonded team can reduce the workload by half. That is why he did not mind the extra time he had to invest in breaking ice and building connections. He was successful in getting the team to back him up without reservations, and the stakeholders too respected his expertise. He knew he had to build his reputation carefully and he couldn't have possibly hit the ground running from the start, so he developed an approach.

As the projects started being assigned, sometimes he had to jump in too deep and other times he would start to get battle ready with at least a few months to gear up.

Charlie says, "There is always one stakeholder that's more important than the rest, learn what he needs and then work backwards. You will have to train them to march to your beat and then it will all become a process. Even your problems will be a part of the process".

This is invaluable advice especially for a PM dealing with a project with many stakeholders, all with varying interests. One should correspond with the stakeholders after preparing an urgency and importance matrix.

What is an urgency and importance matrix?

When there are a lot of pending tasks, one is encouraged to rely on the urgency and importance matrix to decide the order of priority. It relies on the idea that there are a few tasks that are more important while others may not be equally critical. Likewise, there might be tasks that come with a tight deadline. These tasks will be deemed urgent. Now apply this on the stakeholders. If your project concerns the building of a new aircraft, firstly you must get the approval of the organization. It is both urgent and important for the project to kickstart. Secondly, you must gain the approval of the finance department if they have the finance to support the experimentation. Both these stakeholders are urgent and important.

On the other hand, the head of the mechanical team is important for the project but not as urgent as the first two. The existing pilots are neither important nor urgent stakeholders. If a new aircraft gets created, a new crew will automatically be hired to work the additional planes.

The peons and laborers will be the urgent stakeholders because they need to make the working place ready for the new team to congregate and work. However, they are not important since they do not have a strong say in what they want to do or do not want to do. These were just simplified examples of the different stakeholders that may be linked to a project.

From the table below, you can see an intersection of stakeholders who are both important and urgent. They should top your list of priorities. You must follow them with stakeholders that are urgent and not important. Then, you must bring on board the stakeholders who are important but not urgent. Lastly, the stakeholders who are neither important or urgent can be easily cancelled off the list of stakeholders or be dealt with at the very end.

	Important	**Not important**
Urgent	Organization Finance department	Peons
Not urgent	Head of mechanical team	Existing pilots

Enter Caption

Charlie Thompson was a smart project manager. He could recognize and sort his stakeholders in their order of importance. Just as he advised, he always started off by bringing the major stakeholder on board. The rest usually followed with little or no persuasion.

The most important step on a project is to recognize the person who has everyone's reins. That is the person/persons who must be brought on board through a formal or informal channel. Oftentimes these people recognize their own worth and may observe a hard stance during bargaining. As a project manager, you must also be a smart negotiator. If you think you lack somehow in this domain, the obvious advice will be to learn this art. But till then, you may need to bring a strong attorney or a good communication manager on your project team.

A communication manager is an essential position for any project team. If you are heading a big project and dealing with multiple stakeholders, you may downplay the importance of a communication manager but that can become the bane of your project team. Though theoretically it is emphasized that communication in business should be loud and lucid, it is rarely so. It is often brimming with politics and intonations. During such periods, you will realize the importance of a communication specialist. A business attorney can fulfill the same role. If you have a complex project with the possibility of lots of adversaries and hostilities, going without this critical position on your project team can be hazardous. Thus, you should tune your own conversation skills and also get an expert communicator on board.

Your own communication skills will also come in handy in handling the team. Though you will see later that empathy is a crucial trait for a project manager, you may also be needed to use a strict tone at times. You must find a balance in being a boss and a friend. After all, while you want your team to feel at home, you also want them to meet deadlines and deliver on their promises.

Flowserve

Flowserve is another large business that benefited from project management in increasing their labor productivity and decreasing the length of their product cycle. The company that depended on 19000 employees was suffering a managerial crisis when it came to organize and track labor efforts. Thus, they enlisted the help of portfolio and resource management to organize their own workforce.

By installing an automated gate review process, they were able to speed up their production span. Not only did this help increase the total production for the company, but it also reduced the time the products took in getting delivered to the market.

This was another example of how projects planned sensibly with clear tangible or intangible goals in target can benefit the company at large either through improvement in financial statistics, or launch of a new product etc.

Toys"R"Us

As you go about studying examples of poor and effective project management, here is another real-life example. Toys"R"Us is another multinational company, operating in multiple countries across Asia. Its retail outlets add up to 470 stores, situated in Hong Kong, Singapore,

Thailand, China, Japan, Taiwan, Malaysia and Philippines. Its headquarters are based in Hong Kong and until a few years ago, the regional offices were responsible for marketing and E-Commerce. Each country's regional headquarters was responsible for hosting the e-commerce website. However, with a surge in e-commerce and the need for an interactive online presence to replicate or at least resemble the interactive and playful environment of the brands physical shops.

The company enlisted the help of Salesforce for putting up a Commerce Cloud. Now there is one website of Toys"R"Us being managed from Hong Kong while the local marketing teams add their own personalized or customized contribution to the cloud software to cater to their individual audiences. This has cut the cost significantly for the company where earlier each country division was investing in managing the local website. Likewise, the experience on the online platform was also subpar compared to the new unified website since the latter depends on higher level of expertise and greater capitalization. The local teams now focus on regional marketing.

Can you see how Salesforce helped improve the online presence of Toys"R"Us for retail clients across Asia? This became a very critical decision on part of the company as the world was then severely tested by the Covid constraints. They saw a surge in online sales. Also, Thailand did not have a local website earlier, but after a unified website was set up from the headquarters in Hong Kong, Thailand too got an online retail shop.

Julie Adams

If you seek to be successful as a project manager in the modern world, it is critical that you amp up your work strategy. Earlier you might have been an autocratic leader and had a great flourishing career. However, with time you need to fine tune your strategy. The modern world requires leaders that are democratic in their approach.

Today, if you are quick to administer corrections for your team in public, you are likely to lose their confidence and make them rebellious. Self-esteem has become a cardinal component of everyone's identity whether it be the lowest ranking employee in your team. No one will take kindly to the loss of their self-esteem. Be very cautious about being "bossy." A project depends on everyone's cooperation and contribution to be successful.

Julie Adams had been a project manager for the past fifteen years. She had an impressive portfolio where she had supervised projects in multiple firms. She also delivered impressive results. In her resume, she boasted of how she could complete projects before the forecasted deadlines and could oftentimes work within the budget, offering monetary savings to the firms she worked for.

After pursuing her impressive credentials, a major company ABC called her in for a placement. She was immediately rewarded with a project and the upper management kept an eagle's eye on her operations to witness her in action. Within a span of a week, complaints from disgruntled employees started floating up to the upper management. Some complained of overzealous work hours while others complained of extreme interference by the project manager in every domain.

A very old and trusted employee of the firm came forward and put it very succinctly,

"What is the point of appointing overtime from the first day of the project especially since the project is on schedule?"

A major in accounts from a reputed university complained,

"The project manager has opinions about even the most basic things like a debit or credit entry. I feel suffocated under her."

At the meeting with the stakeholders, one stakeholder was quick to point out, "Ms. Adams never allowed her employees to pitch in any input. I could see her team fidgeting with great ideas that they did not word out because she did not allow. In fact, she was quick to take credit for the team's achievement and quicker in laying blame on the team members for any mediocrity."

The upper management too saw these complaints to be true and inferred that the team cannot work cordially towards the goal with such an autocratic leader. They allowed Julie Adams a month as leverage to see if her work tactics evolved but when they found her adamant in her ways, they ended up aborting the contract.

They freed her from her duties by telling her,

"You may have been a very good Project Manager in the past. However, in recent times, companies want a democratic leader who can make the team work cordially towards the target. Over efficiency and perfectionism are no longer the desired traits. It is far more important that everyone on the project stays happy and owns the project. This way every member of the team will deliver their best to the project and the project itself will be successful. Thank you for spending time in our organization but we would like someone else to fill the position of the PM."

From the above scenario you could see that the character traits of a project manager have seen great changes over time. If you have been in the field for long just like Julie Adams, it is likely that you are committing the same blunders. You may be experiencing a fall in your demand because though the profession is experiencing an increasing trend, the qualities sought in a PM have seen a major shift. While earlier, it was believed that an autocratic and forceful leader can better discipline the team and drive efficiency, the circumstances and beliefs have changed in the present. The hiring committee is keen to see if you are kind, considerate and 'empathetic.'

Empathy should be the core character value of a successful project manager. You should be able to view life from the other's perspective. This is very essential if you aim to be a good leader. Your team is not performing well or under-performing. Instead of bringing a cane out, pause and reflect: what may be causing this loss of efficiency?

Is it that the team is ill-suited to the task? Have you inadvertently made the wrong selection of the members? Is one member of the team disruptive or uncooperative in nature?

Maybe you will answer all these questions with a no, but your job does not end here. If you have the right mix of the team members, what may be causing this slump in performance?

Are you failing as a project manager? Are the goals of the project unclear? Have you not allotted responsibility efficiently? Have you overworked your team? Are you keeping expectations far beyond your team's capabilities? Is one of your team members facing a crisis at home that is weighing him down at work?

Does your entire team need a counselling to remain motivated or to find motivation?

If the problem does not even lie here, an empathetic leader will continue to ponder

You may think the workplace is too constrictive and suffocating? Are the working hours getting too long without ample breaks for de-stressing or bonding with colleagues?

Or does your team need a modern project management software like Jira to spur efficiency?

As a leader, and as a leader committed to the team and its goals, you must strive to maintain your team's morale and energy. Your workplace should be brimming with positive energy.

And remember, to keep up with the changes in time, it is imperative that you enlist the help of a project management software. They not only help you organize all your plans, but they will also keep you on your toes by prompting you with time deadlines. They will bind the team by providing live updates on the entire team's performance. Gone are the times of a long chain of hierarchy where each project manager needed to have a bunch of managers under them to overlook the team members from different fields and domains. Now you, as a project manager are the supreme power and the only power in the hierarchy. All your team members will share an equal and vital position under you. This too has become a factor which should compel you to shun the boss within you and to become the "leader'', empathetic and compassionate.

NASA

A good project manager must also ensure that the project team has the skills for the project. These skills refer not only to the qualifications of the team members. You may have hired a very capable team for the project. However, they may not be handy with the project management software. This may sound insane, but this is what happened with a N.A.S.A component a while back. They adopted software for project management but overtime, it reduced efficiency of the team. The project manager complained that the software was showing a divergence in the project plans from what was being proposed by the PM. The team also insisted that the reports processed and produced by the software were either inaccurate or insufficient.

As a result, a software consultant was called in to survey the situation. He interviewed the entire project team and found two problems:

There was a divergence in the people entering the data and the people inferring the data. The data entered did not know how to enter accurate data. Those using the data on the other hand, did not know how to read and process the generated reports. To put it succinctly, the project team was not familiar with the workings of the software.

The second underlying problem was in how the software was fed the project team's breakdown. The project team's breakdown was quite different in actuality from what was fed to the system. You would better understand it with a generic example. Imagine there are three engineers on the team, but the software has been designed with the supposition that there are 5 engineers working round the clock. That means it would always observe the performance of the three engineers based on the prospective efficiency of five engineers. Can you see how it can undermine the performance of the current working members by comparing them to the productive potential of five engineers.

This was somewhat the same problem with the software installed for one of N.A.S. A's project team.

After evaluating and surmising the problem, the consultant proposed a two-day training workshop for the project team on how to use the software. The workshop gave a comprehensive guide on how to enter data in the software and how to read the reports being generated by the program. It also highlighted the benefits of using the project management software. Not only this, but the presenter also illustrated cases which may indicate out-of-control or unfavorable reports. It also explained how to deal with these situations in order to control them and mitigate the losses.

The project manager also organized another session on the basics of project management. That session taught concepts like what is project management? What are the essential traits for a project team? How should the project team work together? It also taught the different phases of project management. In short, it delivered the same training to the N.A.S.A project team that you gained through this book. Can you now appreciate the importance of this book in your path for becoming a successful project manager?

After all this training, the team was able to successfully use the software to improve their efficiency and keep track of the complexities of the project. Does this example remind you of the equation of success you studied in chapter 3?

People + Processes = success and innovation

As a project manager, if you have implemented modern processes at your workplace but fail to provide training to your "people," you will be stranded on the journey. Efficient processes without trained personnel are like a wasted investment. Thus, in your seeking of modernization, ensure that you keep everyone in the team at pace with you. Systems need people to operate them. Software needs people to make data entry and only then, can an efficient software deliver accurate and refined results. Remember this equation to achieve "success and innovation."

KiwiRail

KiwiRail is a national enterprise responsible for managing the railway network within New Zealand and adjoining islands. Some time back, it wanted to close one of its factories responsible for providing replacement parts and repair services. This was a complex plan and needed a proper project manager team to execute the facility closure without causing a hindrance in the railway commute.

The Carawel project was assigned the task of closing the factory without any bumps and jerks. It had a comprehensive list of tasks to achieve:

1. It had to sell all the complex machinery at the factory. They had to find interested candidates for the sale of whole or parts of the machinery and secure the best bargain.

2. It had to look into ensuring that the existing workforce was amicably replaced and freed of the contract without any legal complications. It meant negotiating with the trade unions, providing salaries in advance for terminating the contracts, and finding the employees good replacements in the work market.

3. The project team also had to ensure that since one of the factories was closing up, there should be no hurdles in the delivery of replacement and repair parts to the railway network, disrupting the transportation facility in any way.

4. The project team was also responsible for closing off the accounts of machinery and parts that remained unsold, without any prospective clients. They had to ensure that these inventories and assets are disposed of or discarded efficiently, securing the highest gains possible.

Thus, the project team exhibited impressive skills in closing the project while delivering all the goals and tasks within the agreed deadline and budget. This was just an example of the complexities of the project in the modern world. These projects often have multiple facets and need a specialized and committed team to rise to the challenge. Such complex tasks cannot be completed by the in-house team of an organization alone. These projects can extend for months and cost millions of dollars, but the only other alternative is to let the task scatter for years and remain unaccomplished or unsorted, while a million dollars still go to waste.

Caroline Sams

Until now, you have got a good understanding of what your job as a project manager entails. You also saw multiple examples of successful and unsuccessful project management. If you are an avid reader, you must have already made a checklist of things to do and red flags to avoid.

If you have done this, you are a smart project manager. You have added years of experience to your portfolio by reading this book alone. You are likely to remain safe from a multiple of problems that many new project managers make in their course of learning. Here is another precious piece of advice for you from the books of Caroline Sams.

She says her professor at grad school used this tactic with the students that she later deployed on her team. She said that her professor used to end the class by asking these questions from each student directly,

- "What problem are you facing?"
- "Where are you slowing down?"
- "Which topic do you want me to explain again?"

She says this round of questioning was often followed by eager feedback, where each student divulged his trouble spots. She says this scenario was the exact opposite of what happened in all the other classes.

All the other professors used to end their sessions with a general question targeted at the whole class, "was the lecture clear?"

This question was often followed by half-hearted nods and mumbled responses. Rarely did any student come up with a query. The shy lot in the class considered this as the ripe opportunity for observing the polish on their shoes and the dirt on their toenails.

Caroline Sams says I practiced both the questioning tactics with my project team. When I posed a generalized question to the whole lot of them, there was hardly ever any feedback. It never meant that the project was sailing all smooth. It usually meant that every team member was hesitant in bringing the attention all to themselves.

When she engaged in individualized questioning and in-depth probes, she often got a lot of queries. It also improved the generalized atmosphere of the project team where everybody learnt that having problems and difficulties was not a taboo. It was the process of collective learning. The team also bonded well where they each brainstormed on solutions of their teammates. Sams reports then occasionally, her team started interjecting with the questions with their own initiative. She had inculcated an environment of learning and acceptance.

She thinks this is an important tactic that should be followed by project managers worldwide because it removes half the hurdles from the project. If such an environment does not flourish, the team members will clutch their problems to their bosom and commit to resolve them on their own, because of which the project could get into a lurch in the future.

So, this was another crucial piece of advice for you and hopefully you have scribbled it down in your notebook. Do practice this stream of questioning in your next project meeting and you will be astounded by the amount of information it uncovers. If you think rounds of individual questioning carried out in group meetings can be time-consuming, you can time it for once-a-month meetings. The rest of the days you could go round your project team and ask them personally. Instead of a general "what are you up to?" ask "what are your problems, where are you getting stuck, where do you need my help?" your team needs you whether you know it or not.

Be the project manager your team can rely on. Be their savior. You have all the skills to uphold this mantle with grace and dignity.

CHAPTER EIGHT

EXTRAS

Enter Caption

Businesses aren't limited to one or two projects at a time. Managers juggle people, goals, and tasks daily with the pressure of ensuring that every project is successful. All projects are an effort to add value to the company through a service or product. The team has met the set of needs, and the project manager ensures the process is smooth throughout. Each project is unique and is likely to differ from the ongoing activities of an organization. However, managing projects without external help or electronic solutions can be time-consuming for the company and affect the team's performance.

Recently Aramco Head of I.T. reported that the company could save $1million by implementing SAP Cloud to boost their business operations and employee experience.

He reported that the company was facing a considerable challenge in process efficiency because earlier, they were relying on standard software and avoiding customization. He further revealed that the company reduced its application management time to 50% after adopting the cloud.

The new software helped the company gain more visibility in its industry. Its primary functions of H.R., finance, and the vendor also smoothly transitioned into a more effective and fast process. Their I.T. maintenance reduced their expenses and improved employee satisfaction greatly. And they expect the R.O.I. on the investment to be lucrative.

According to the C.E.O. Aramco, the company has significantly increased efficiency across Europe, Africa, and Asia. Their move to the intelligent suit in the cloud has given the company users ease to perform daily activities faster and from anywhere in the world. The managers felt more respected for their opinions and informed of the costs of their services.

Jane was an IT PM and required a consulting company to develop the feasibility of moving their customer relationship management using Salesforce.

It was Monday morning, and Jane entered the office with a frowning forehead. Most likely, she was upset because of the coffee stains that got her newly white shirt messy. She joined the meeting room and sat down at her favorite place near the window, facing her head downwards.

Mr. Jackson was the business strategist hired by the firm to brief on the benefits of "implementing Salesforce.'

He started, "Hello everyone! welcome to the new world of technology and data analytics."

He continued detailing the software and summarized his presentation in his conclusion, saying, "this system will make operations simple and increase job satisfaction for all business users of customers across the board."

The key to effective project management is efficiency in all aspects of the project. If you don't use all resources at your disposal, you're likely to do more work than necessary. As a project manager, you have the liberty to use project management software that makes it easier to keep track of who is working on what. Especially if teams collaborate across projects via inefficient email threads or chat software, that can lead to missed deadlines or dissatisfied clients.

Remember, the success of a project depends on how well it's managed; thus, using project management systems to help you stay organized while working and executing projects should be a top priority in an organization's budget.

Imagine this,

You are a project manager for a non-governmental organization that works to empower women from rural areas of the country. The organization has multiple projects running throughout the year with varying deadlines. As a project manager, you're working for the women and children's health program. You have a team of workers who look at the project's different aspects but work together to ensure all key indicators are met. As a manager, you need to effectively plan your project, respond to problems, manage available resources, and ensure that all stakeholders are involved in the project. The essential functions of project management involve the 5 phases of project management and should be consulted for.

Project managers use several tools, approaches, and techniques to satisfy the needs of the project. One of the critical tools to use is **PM (project management) software**. The primary purpose of PM software is to assist managers like yourself through different stages in your project.

Suppose you have to schedule visits, it requires more than just looking into your team's work schedule. You have to make reservations for a place to stay and other logistical needs assigned to someone to oversee and ensure they don't miss any detail. Then, what are the goals that need to be met during this visit? Where is all the data collected stored and managed after the visit? The software helps to unite team collaboration, management of resources, billing, and finance, etc. Every little detail that can be relevant to your project should be managed through an electronic system.

Benefits of a PM software

To eliminate chances of human error and reduce work time, using an efficient project management system can help you stay organized at work when you're executing a project or planning a new one.

1. Improved Resource Management

PM software are successful tools because they help manage resources effectively. This isn't limited to financial resources but everything and everyone you have onboard for the project. Are you at the risk of overbooking? Have you committed to the deadline that you will not be able to meet? You can easily avoid such mishaps and have a smooth sailing project using software that helps outline resources used and when they will be used. You can also calculate the cost of the usage and pick out resource bottlenecks. Effective resource management promotes a healthier work environment for your team.

2. Efficient Project Planning

The most critical part of project management is planning and scheduling everything. Without a timeline in front of you, it can get tricky for your team to stay on track and within the project deadline. The lack of set guidelines can be highly damaging to your progress in the project, and precious time is lost when employees report to work without knowing the tasks that need to be done.

Not only does the lack of structure to a project affect the overall team productivity, but you're also going to find it challenging to communicate tasks between groups. PM software is a great tool to outline duties and highlight them. You can also set deadlines, schedule visits, prevent miscommunication, and have everything consolidated in one place, so there is easier access for you and your team.

3. Documentation

Documentation is at the heart of any project and extremely time-sensitive to deal with. Many businesses make use of PM software solely for data collection, management, and storage. If you're still using spreadsheets or pen and paper to keep track of your team's progress, you're likely going to exhaust yourself and deal with potential errors eventually. A PM software ensures that data-based documentation is accurate. This means all kinds of data, from bills, a list of vendors, project resources, upcoming calendar events, key indicators, completed tasks, to scheduled visits. Plus, all of these are arranged so that they are easily accessible to retrieve and view.

4. Effective Team Communication and Collaboration

It is challenging to ensure the success of a project if the team working towards its completion doesn't communicate well with each other. PM software is designed to improve team collaboration. As a manager, you delegate tasks to your team members individually, making up a part of a larger goal, i.e., project completion. The software ensures that no communication is lost between team members and gives them a platform to collaborate on smaller projects through dynamic discussions, timelines, and outstanding tasks. The team feels like a part of a larger project, and members know what everyone is doing individually.

Of course, using project management software is a step towards a practical completion of tasks for you and easier management of the data and your team. This brings the eventual question, i.e., what approach should one take towards the selection process? Is PM software just as good as a standardized selection process? How do you know which one fits your project the best?

There have been teams of more than 50 people who spent two years on a selection process for a project. They developed a specific selection criterion where vendors were called to present their cases, shortlisted products were tested, and the candidates approved underwent a strict selection process through levels management.

On the other hand, an individual with little to no knowledge of the project, product, or application could select a PM software. Either option is an extreme that is not going to work for you. A selection team can review dozens of candidates against a strict selection criterion and still chooses to develop an in-house project management tool. This only wastes more time and talent of the company that could be utilized for other projects and tasks that promote the company's vision.

The key here is to find a middle-ground solution that works out for everyone in the company. Now, this starts with selecting a project management software with team effort.

Consider Cairn Oil & Gas, a subsidiary of Vedanta Limited, transformed their business functions by ERP implantation. The company's objective was to improve its production output to some five hundred thousand barrels, and its domestic share in the market is somewhere close to 50%. The company aimed to shorten its accounting records and end-of-year closing by choosing a better ERP than its traditional in-house software.

The company started from SAP basic application to SAP S/4HANA to SAP Fiori user experience for mobile supported transactions and applications for producing financial reports like trial balance, budgets, and asset balances. Their decision-making improved highly as the dashboard updated them about their consumed and available budgets and their turnaround time to produce close financial reports also got faster.

Cairn believes their future growth will be drastic as it estimated their productivity increased by 12-25%. They were now able to report their intercompany consolidation earlier, and their response time quintupled. They were also able to get business insight by built-in analytics for operational glitches like slow-moving inventory items.

Another giant company-based Tacoma, Washington True blue, employed Oracle Cloud application, and their I.T. team bandwidth drastically increased. They were able to divert their energies to newer and more lucrative projects.

True blue connects employers with approximately 700,000 people annually. The company was facing trouble in its online portal providing staffing, workforce management, and recruitment process.

Although their information needs were unique, Oracle H.C.M. Cloud and Oracle ERP cloud met them at the right place, and now the system supports them to fill a job within 9 seconds while the employer companies can now place orders for talent hunt on need basis using a smartphone from anywhere in the world 24/7.

Everything on the portal is real-time, from job orders being fulfilled to connecting to the potential candidates to even supporting them to do their payroll faster.

Choosing a Software

If you're working with a team of professionals on a project, they will likely want to be kept informed about decisions you make and even take part in the selection process of these decisions. With thousands of tools on the market, finding the best project management tool for your team can be daunting. Too often, team leaders buy a project management tool only to discover that they're the only ones using it in a few months. When comparing tools, remember that an effective project management tool should satisfy two main requirements: First, it should have all the features that a project manager needs. Second, the tool should be something your entire team is willing to use.

Satisfying both requirements is easier said than done, so, these essential steps ensure your team finds the best project management tool for your needs. Are you ready to get organized?

- Define your project management tool needs.
- Research the best project management tools.
- Test out the tool.

- Get feedback from your team.
- Evaluate the cost.
- Get executive buy-in.
- Purchase the project management tool.
- Implement the project management tool.
- Analyze with a retrospective.

Similarly, when choosing a PM software, remember that it is better through team effort. If you have a team of 3 to 6 key players that depend on the stakeholders' contribution, they will need some consensus amongst the stakeholders, if not all, for this selection process. However, you're going to consider the input of all stakeholders so they understand that their opinions are valued. Including team members and stakeholders in the selection process is a great way to let them know that they are part of a process that affects them.

While it is difficult to get the input of all stakeholders during the decision process and almost impossible to satisfy everyone involved, asking for their input and making them feel included is already an excellent way for you to build the foundation for eventual success. It is a general behavioral response to accept decisions if you make someone feel involved and included. However, on the opposite end, if you don't include them in the decision-making process, you're likely to see more opposition than necessary simply because their input was not taken into consideration. Thus, try and avoid a situation where you might have to deal with rejection based on such grounds and try to seek opinions of the process from as many stakeholders and team members as you can.

Tip:

1. When selecting a PM software, keep in mind the larger picture and consider the connectivity to other systems.

2. Make sure you're avoiding any political decisions like choosing a tool or product simply because you're going to feel less criticized for your selection if, at any point, it fails as a solution.

3. Find a middle-ground between the operations functions and projects.

Budget-Saving Tip: The cost of the software shouldn't be the first thing that you consider when you're selecting a PM tool. Mainly because they do not make up a large percentage of the project's costs; however, there are running costs of the software. For example, how much will it cost to run the software for maybe five years? What about the hardware upgrades and the training? These are minor details that eventually catch up on the budget and need to be considered before deciding to get any PM tool.

However, the most important thing to keep in mind is what you want to accomplish with the software, thus what features will work the best for you. Look for that perfect balance between the accessibility/user-friendliness and features of the software.

Tips for Software Selection

- Learn about the features and functions offered by the software and select the business process model that meets your business needs.

- Take all the steps to connect the software features to specific business processes that could benefit the overall business objectives

- Reach a consensus among stakeholders about the most important software features and integrate them to ease out processes for all stakeholders

- Make sure to follow the scope and stay within budget by ensuring focus

- Develop a custom demo for all your stakeholder's business needs for vendors to follow.

Implementing the Software

The next step to choosing software is the successful "*Implementation of the software,*" so selecting software is only a tool; real diligence is needed to understand the process and the role of people in the process to ensure commitment to ensure the computer-based project management success.

First, take a look at what can be accomplished with PM software apart from its features in detail. You can achieve efficient data management, provide a user interface, manage your schedules and communicate better. Each area listed above is critical to any project's success. If any feature is found lacking, you're going to face hurdles in the future and the present, as well as waste resources. The importance of each key factor is discussed previously in the "Benefits of a PM software" section.

So, what do you need to begin with?

In order to implement the PM software of your choice to run smoothly throughout the project, the two things that will help in the process;

- Dedication to providing quality
- Training

Remember, any project management tool is not an easy ride for anyone who has just been introduced. You should expect your team members to plan to learn the tool; this can be a long process for some. However, the key is to speak of the spirit and train everyone properly so there isn't any miscommunication in the future.

Dedication to providing quality

As a project management team, if your goal is clear and you find yourself dedicated from the start, nothing can hinder your success in implementing the software for your project management needs. You will have to consider having a project manager who is highly motivated and embarks upon the journey with leadership qualities. Not only will he be able to inspire the learning in his team, but he will also be able to bring about the radical change technology has brought about.

If you are an old project team in the market, you need to work with a growth mindset and an improvised set of skills to survive and compete with the new entrants.

What do you think "Salesforce Einstein" brought for the project teams?

Faster and better task performance

And what do you think was the objective of their project manager?

They had a dedication to provide quality and innovation.

Therefore, as a project manager, it's of utmost importance to meet the growing demands and stay updated to the modern world.

Take a look around you, from mobiles to various devices of daily use; everything is now connected, companies are being restructured to meet the needs of higher efficiency and productivity.

Open your phone, and you will see Amazon bringing artificial intelligence into your homes through the intelligent voice server of Alexa and Polly. While Alexa helps you operate your phones, Polly develops and supports applications that improve accessibility and efficiency in businesses by giving you dozens of options to convert text to speech and improve mechanized responses.

As project managers, therefore, in the case of technology, you need to adapt to tools that offer the best "R.O.I."

So, the question is, 'How should the project manager promise to deliver quality?'

As a go-to process, the project manager should take the challenge head-on and develop the skills required for the rapid changes. They should build an understanding of the problems in the environment and be a catalyst to organizational changes. They should work towards developing a stronger team. A project manager must develop a model to plan and check its teams' skills and work to provide quality and innovation.

Beath (1991) was an expert in I.T., and he identified an approach for the future project managers;

"He called out for expertise, innovation and the need to be a change agent."

As a project manager, you must use your authority to implement and negotiate the challenges of people and the environment that come along while implementing software.

Say, for instance, you identified that the problem is that the team is ill-equipped and needs training on using the highly digitalized ERP or Cloud-based system. You will have to nip it in the bud and help the team work on their skills and observe if your team is practicing the learned skills on the ground. Remember, your team can become your biggest hurdle in implementing a top-notch tool, or they could be your weapon and strength.

At an individual level, a project manager should instill a passion for 'Conscious learning' in people, be a catalyst to support "organizational change," and seek to "assist" the business environment. Of course, you should have a proactive attitude, a growth mindset, and a desire to learn and bring a change.

Remember, once you align your mind and develop an approach, everything else that follows will become easy to accomplish. So, gear up to unlearn and learn and relearn during the process. For the successful implantation, the skills would range from conflict management to willingness to adapt to computer and software skills to respecting each other for collective performance. But would it be possible if the project manager themselves failed? No

So you will have to work on yourself more than work on others, and for that, you will have to revisit your learnings from the chapter on "Vision setting."

Take a look at these pointers to help you through and through in implementing the software with an innovative mind;

- Take responsibility for your actions
- Check your methods
- Be open to changes
- Align your methodologies with the project objectives
- Take support from top management, sponsor (anyone who supports your dedication and innovation)

Once you start working towards innovation, you will be able to considerably enhance the benefits of project management software by integrating functions that support other functions. So this will help you avoid redundancy and wasteful resources and create synergies.

- Look for common data points; labels, and pigeonholes to connect the data between subsystems
- Give rewards to your team
- Issue new and detailed job descriptions and eliminate duplication of responsibilities
- Try to integrate the software that connects other management systems like finance and H.R. also.

Remember, when you are trying to implement the software, the roles and duties of project management should not be confused with functional responsibilities, and it's advisable to have separate individuals for both.
  • Be a project leader and not a functional leader

- Be knowledgeable so project participants can take inspiration and learn from you.
- Learn to delegate tasks with clear expectations

Training

After you've selected software that is approved by many and meets the criteria for your project, naturally, the next step is learning how to use it before you implement it. This is where the training phase of your PM tool selection process starts. The training process is divided into two parts,
  1- PM software Training
  2- Project Management Training
You cannot start PM software training without having basic PM training. Without the full knowledge of what program planning entails, your team members are likely not to use all the software features correctly and increase the workload instead. Everyone involved in the project's success needs to have appropriate knowledge and training in the basic idea of project management. There will be instances where you're going to collaborate with individuals who might not understand what project management is, and to expect that of them is unfair, to begin with. The wider audience should have access to a program covering an enormous

scope of topics that add value to their project management knowledge. It should be a program that ensures everyone understands that project management is a skill that will be used frequently in the company. Every employee ought to familiarize themselves with it.

Tip: The program should highlight that the company is firm about everyone attending these sessions to learn more about PM and eventually implement it through a PM software to the specific projects they are working on. You can start with getting your corporate training function involved.

If they are skilled and have the resources, it is only fair to ask them to participate in the sessions. If not, they might show dissatisfaction with you and create unnecessary hurdles for you and your team.

Training individuals for PM also includes teaching them how to use the PM tools available, specifically PM software. The use of tools may vary according to the job description of a person. For example, a user community that feeds information into the system and one that uses and responds to the information is divided according to their roles. The former must understand the basics of planning and how their input affects the system's results.

As for the latter, they are tasked with understanding how the resulting information due to the input was determined. This requires the team to have the ability to interpret and respond to the information correctly. They are to be trained, so they don't just issue reports to provide the status of the program, instead use it to identify any upcoming risks and propose a corrective measure soon after. Thus, training is vital for people to read reports, identify issues, and respond to any untoward situation.

When you're at the implementing stage of the training, this is the time that you identify all recipients of the outputs, and it will help you determine what all they need to know when learning the software. After you have their job descriptions with you, start by designing custom outputs for each individual to carry out their part of the project easily. After designing these reports, you can ensure that all of them learn their responsibilities in the project, so there is no room for confusion later on. Just remember, this isn't you spoon-feeding your team; instead, you need to make sure that each participant knows how to respond to problems, what to look for, and be effective in their specific roles.

A barrage of information about the whole project might be overwhelming for many. Thus employing this method to spread out only relevant information to each team member is a great way to ensure the project's success. You can even formally introduce this training as a certified program, either sponsored externally or internally.

Project Management Tools

Project management has always been practiced throughout history, both formally and informally. As it began to emerge as a recognized profession, researchers streamlined the processes. It became evident that PM tools are a great way to make project management more efficient. Thus, with the motivation to address the needs of proper scheduling, resource allotment, and potential risks, they designed standardized tools for project management. These tools make your life as a project manager more straightforward, and they also help new team members become comfortable with managing their specific roles in the project. With technological advancements long gone are the days of spreadsheets or using pen and paper to record and organize the project's progress. Instead, PM software has become extremely popular within all fields, be it an I.T. company, an N.G.O., or a corporate setting.

Of course, not all software works for all kinds of projects; thus, as a project manager, it is your job to find software with features that work best for your project. Here is a list of a few well-known PM software used across a wide variety of fields.

Jira

Jira is one of the most popular software project managers use for workflow management systems, particularly in the I.T. industry. It is a prevailing tool that makes tackling big projects a breeze. The software serves project teams to apply the tools for agile project management methodology easily.

From traditional PM to generating I.T. tickets, the software provides a comprehensive system for project planning, reporting, organizing teams, and creating projects. Here is a list of few features that make the software best to meet your needs;

It seamlessly allows you to customize workflows according to your project needs so you can easily transition from a completed task to a review stage or an in-progress task to the completion stage.

It offers several options for reporting to help visualize project progress, workload, and project bottlenecks too.

Its automation engine helps project managers to define instructions for automated actions. For instance, a project manager can define an auto email instruction on task completions, etc.

Workzone

Workzone is software built with extreme dedication to helping teams and individuals in an organization improve your control on all projects and increase visibility in work management. It is used as a shared workspace online for everyone to collect and communicate while giving you the control to manage and share work, so everyone remains updated on the phase of the project.

A few features of Workzone that stand out are,

- It helps with seamless communication between team members

- Great for creating to-do lists, task lists, schedules, and sharing files.

- It gives control to managers to set permissions for different users, even allowing visibility for clients.

- You can get reports regularly, so everyone knows where the project is lagging and where they have been doing relatively well.

Proofhub

Proofhub is one of the most popular PM software being widely used in multiple industries. Its versatility allows leading organizations like Disney, NASA, etc., to prefer it over any other software. It is dubbed an all-in-one tool with a large variety of features so that you don't have to look for other complementary software or tools to make sure your project runs smoothly.

The company came up with a work-from-home module that allows teams to communicate electronically with a 100% cloud-enabling feature. It lets all employees log into a single project management tool for all their project needs. Plus, the data is secure as the software has a secured I.P. feature that lets you restrict I.P. addresses.

Proofhub works wonderfully as a task manager in a detailed and organized manner. Everything, starting from the task's due date to files and billed time, is mentioned with every task. This way, team members always have the context to every task before tackling it. Similarly, it has an efficient communication system across team members with features like one-on-one chat, group chat, and task comments.

You can also get insight into how well your project has been doing, whether your team is productive throughout, and if the task deadlines are being met regularly. It highlights any potential risks for going off track from your proposed project completion deadline, so you can take measures and adjust the tasks accordingly.

Proprofs

Proprofs is a project management tool popular for having a simple interface, with ample features as project management tools. The software is designed for various businesses, regardless of how big or small they are. As a project manager, you'll find Proprofs perfect for your needs because it brings all your projects under one roof and allows you to designate tasks for your teams according to their projects.

The software is efficient for communication across teams allowing them to share files on the go, have discussions and leave comments/feedback on tasks, and use the chat box for any confusions or roadblocks to figure out. You can easily manage the progress of the projects, schedule deadlines, and allow team members to look at the bigger picture when they are working on their particular tasks. You can also create timesheets for all members, manage billable hours and overtime.

General Tips for Project Managers

As a PM, you've likely had your fair share of risks and successes that add to your experience. Project management is a skill that is becoming increasingly relevant for all organizations and happens to be a requirement for many who are looking to increase their efficiency and timeliness at work.

While we've already discussed some of the official responsibilities of project managers previously, there are still some tips and tricks in the market that will help you feel more at ease as a beginner, or if you're a seasoned manager, these will prove as a great reminder.

- Have an end goal in mind as you begin a project. Having a vision for what you want out of a project isn't always limiting. Experts say that having a specific starting and ending point is a marker for a successful project. A consistent reminder of your end goal keeps you in check during the goal completion. Plus, to streamline it further, you can use a PM software as a tool to keep your end goal in sight.

- Risk management is one of the most critical skills of a project manager. Identify an issue and work towards a risk-response strategy. Imagine something as simple as this, and if you can't work as well in the mornings as you do at night, maybe you can plan your day so that you get enough rest throughout the day to work and be productive at night.

- Wanting everything to work out just the way you planned can be frustrating and mentally taxing. One of the most important tips given by experts is to avoid perfectionism when taking ownership of a project. There are situations and factors out of your control. Instead of focusing on them and potentially derailing the progress of your whole team, look for a workaround. You can even focus on simply meeting the project's predetermined goals instead of ensuring that everything is perfect. Usually, the completed project is likely to meet the overall expectations of its stakeholders, and you're going to have a successful project to boast about!

References

Forbes (2017). How happy employees make happy customers. Available online at https://www.forbes.com/sites/shephyken/2017/05/27/how-happy-employees-make-happy-customers/?sh=7390c1be5c35

A Brief Note About The Author

Rohit Romley is a Salesforce project manager and a business analyst. He Is known for energizing businesses, IT organizations, and supplier networks to visualize the value and impact of technology, formulate strategies and then commit and execute on delivering changes that bring meaningful results for customers, employees and to the top and bottom line.

Through this book, he has laid emphasis on empathy as it plays an important role when managing client as well as employee relationships.

Queries/feedback: rohit@pixeledapps.com